REAL JUSTICE:

YOUNG, INNOCENT AND IN PRISON

• • •

THE STORY OF ROBERT BALTOVICH

JEFF MITCHELL

JAMES LORIMER & COMPANY LTD., PUBLISHERS
TORONTO

James Lorimer & Company Ltd., Publishers, acknowledges the support of the Ontario Arts Council. We acknowledge the financial support of the Government of Canada through the Canada Book Fund for our publishing activities. We acknowledge the support of the Canada Council for the Arts which last year invested $24.3 million in writing and publishing throughout Canada. We acknowledge the Government of Ontario through the Ontario Media Development Corporation's Ontario Book Initiative.

Canada Council
for the Arts

ONTARIO ARTS COUNCIL
CONSEIL DES ARTS DE L'ONTARIO

Library and Archives Canada Cataloguing in Publication

Mitchell, Jeff
    Real justice : young, innocent and in prison : the story of Robert Baltovich / Jeff Mitchell.

(Real justice)
Includes bibliographical references and index.
Issued also in electronic format.
ISBN 978-1-4594-0079-5 (bound).--ISBN 978-1-4594-0078-8 (pbk.)

    1. Baltovich, Robert. 2. Bain, Elizabeth, d. 1990. 3. Murder-- Ontario-- Scarborough--Juvenile literature. 4. Judicial error-- Ontario--Scarborough--Juvenile literature. I. Title.

HV6535.C33S38 2012   j364.152'309713541   C2011-908691-3

James Lorimer & Company Ltd.,
Publishers
317 Adelaide Street West, Suite 1002
Toronto, ON, Canada
M5V 1P9
www.lorimer.ca

Distributed in the United States by:
Orca Book Publishers
P.O. Box 468
Custer, WA, USA
98240-0468

Printed and bound in Canada.
Manufactured by Friesens Corporation in Altona, Manitoba, Canada in February 2012
Job #72999

FOR CAROLYN AND GEORGE MITCHELL

CONTENTS

	Foreword	7
1	Rob and Liz	13
2	Falling in Love	16
3	Missing	23
4	A Terrible Discovery	30
5	"We think you did it."	35
6	The Police Build Their Case	41
7	Under Arrest	46
8	Rob's Case Goes to Court	51
9	The Trial Begins	55
10	Cracks in the Case	67
11	The Verdict	72
12	Prison	77
13	A Tragedy at Home	85
14	James Lockyer	89
15	Building a New Case	95
16	Paul Bernardo	99
17	Proven Innocent	105
18	Questions Linger	110
	Afterword	116
	Acknowledgements	119
	Where Are They Now?	120
	Timeline	121
	Glossary	123
	Further Reading	125
	Photo Credits	126
	Index	127

Think for a moment about yourself. About where you are in life.

What is important to you? What makes you happy?

What do you expect from life? What do you wish for?

For many of us, the answers to those questions are quite simple. We place importance on the things closest to us. Family and friends. The activities we enjoy. School and studies. Sports and music.

We may not think about it a lot, but we come to expect things to be a certain way. We live in our homes and go to school. We spend time with family and friends. All very ordinary.

You likely expect to complete school and go on to work at a career you enjoy. You may have a dream job in mind. Someday, maybe you'll have a family of your own. We all want a happy, peaceful life.

But what if something changed all that? What if something far beyond your control brought your life to a sudden stop?

That was what happened to Robert Baltovich. Growing up in Toronto, Rob was ordinary in every way. He loved his family and friends. He enjoyed school and sports. He never got into the kind of trouble that would attract the attention of the police.

In 1990, Rob was in his early twenties and a student at the University of Toronto. He studied hard. He took time to enjoy life, too. He was probably a lot like you.

And he was in love with a beautiful girl. He hoped they would someday be married.

Suddenly, Rob's life became a nightmare. His girlfriend, Elizabeth Bain, went missing. The police believed she was murdered. And they thought that Rob was the killer.

Imagine being blamed for the worst kind of crime. Imagine being innocent, but being seen by the whole world as guilty. Imagine feeling that no matter how often you tell the truth, it just won't matter. No one seems to believe you.

That was Rob's experience. And it only got worse.

Rob Baltovich was found guilty of killing Liz. He was sent to prison, despite insisting that he was innocent. He had to fight for years to clear his name.

Other innocent people have been sent to jail. Their stories stand out because of the circumstances involved. Some have been very young, or very poor. Some have been the victims of racism.

Rob was not especially young, or poor. He wasn't affected by racism. But he was caught up in a system that convicted him and sent him—the wrong person—to jail.

Rob was an ordinary person caught up in an extraordinary situation. It changed his life forever. His story shows that what happened to him could happen to any of us.

It's also a story of how a normal person can find remarkable strength. And a story of how all of us have the power to make things right, if we have the courage to try.

PROLOGUE

Yonge Street in Toronto is noisy with traffic on a sunny summer afternoon. Robert Baltovich exits a public library and begins to walk south. He blends in easily with the hundreds of people on the sidewalk. This is his city, where he was born and raised, where he has lived most of his life. Lean and fit, his eyes hidden by sunglasses and a knapsack over his shoulder, he looks like other people enjoying their freedom on this fine day.

Perhaps of the dozens of people who will pass him and see his face, a few will recognize Rob. He is known for being accused and convicted in the early 1990s of the murder of his girlfriend, Elizabeth Bain. And he is famous for having proven, after many years in prison and a long legal fight, that he is innocent of that crime.

Rob Baltovich's case is one of the most high-profile examples of wrongful conviction in Canada's history.

He is mentioned along with David Milgaard, Steven Truscott, and Donald Marshall, all men who were put in jail for crimes they did not commit. Rob was in his mid-twenties when the life he knew was stopped short. He had just finished university and was looking forward to a normal life. He expected to find a good job, get married, have kids, and enjoy years of freedom and choice.

But everything changed when Elizabeth, the girl he was in love with, went missing in the spring of 1990. He found himself frantically searching for the woman he had hoped to marry. His distress deepened when it became clear Elizabeth had been abducted and killed.

Rob found himself living a nightmare when the police and the public thought he was responsible for what had happened to Liz.

Rob's life has been a journey from despair to redemption. Almost twenty years of his young life have been plagued by suspicion, prosecution, and prison. Despite that, today he is an upbeat and hopeful man. While one might expect anger and bitterness, Rob is peaceful and thoughtful about his ordeal.

"I argue with the idea that my life was taken from me. If I had my life to live over again I would prefer this had not happened. But the fact is, I don't think any of us really know the direction our life is going to take," Rob said in July of 2009.

"In some ways I think it made me a wiser person; it made me a more compassionate person. But at the same time, I've had a lot taken away from me. But nobody has a perfect life."

Today, Rob is asked to speak to the public about issues of justice — and injustice — in this country. His message is that he was an ordinary man swept up in a most unusual circumstance. He thinks this message is important for young people.

"I was not really much different than they are. It's something that could happen to someone and to everyone," Rob said. "I also tell them the chances of it happening are very remote. But the fact is, it did happen."

Rob Baltovich's story can teach us many lessons. Some are obvious: when the legal system goes wrong, we are all affected. But on another level, Rob's story is one of courage and strength, of enduring horrible circumstances and emerging as a better person.

And it is a story of fighting, despite the obstacles along the way, for what is right.

$$1$$

CHAPTER ONE

ROB AND LIZ

"Oh, wow!" Robert Baltovich said. "You see that girl? She's beautiful!"

It was a fine summer day in 1987. Rob sat in the passenger seat of a Weed Man truck as it rattled along a street in Toronto. Rob turned his head to watch a slender woman with gleaming black hair. She was jogging along the sidewalk, wearing a pink tank top and shorts. She was the most beautiful girl he had ever seen.

Rob was twenty-two years old. He had a landscaping job between semesters as a psychology student at the University of Toronto. He lived with his mom, Adele, and his dad, Jim, who ran a convenience store. From an early age, Rob had helped out around the store, stocking shelves and spending time with his dad.

Rob was born and raised in Scarborough, in the east end of Toronto. He was an active, athletic guy who loved to read. He liked hanging out with his buddies, working out at the gym, and spending sunny days at the beach on Lake Ontario.

Rob was self-confident and independent. He was good at a wide range of pursuits, including music, drama, sports, and school. He had plenty of friends and a close family. He was a young man looking forward to what life had in store for him. The sight of the beautiful young woman jogging along the street made him pause and smile.

As the girl ran off, Rob turned to his friend who was steering the truck along the tree-lined street.

"Man," he said. "Why don't I ever meet anybody like that?"

As summer gave way to fall, the image of the girl he'd seen jogging that day stayed with him, even as his classes at U of T resumed. So Rob was amazed when one day he saw her again. She was in a school hallway, chatting with classmates. She wore a red dress and again dazzled Rob with her beauty.

Wow, he thought. *She is stunning.*

"I just couldn't take my eyes off her," Rob said many years later as he recalled the moment.

She was a dark-eyed beauty whose striking looks came from her parents. Her mom was from the Philippines and her dad of Scottish and Italian descent, raised in Argentina. Some guys might have felt shy about approaching such a pretty girl, but Rob was so attracted by her beauty and grace that he felt he had to speak to her.

"She just looked like a really, really nice girl — and incredibly beautiful," he said.

After class, Rob approached the young woman and got right to the point.

"Hi, I'm Rob," he said. "Would you like to have lunch with me sometime?"

"Sure," she said, smiling.

Rob at last learned her name: Elizabeth Bain.

2

CHAPTER TWO

FALLING IN LOVE

Rob and Liz started spending a lot of time together. Liz was new to the school. She had recently transferred from U of T's downtown campus. She lived nearby in Scarborough with her parents, sister, and two brothers. She had few friends, and was grateful for Rob's friendship.

Rob found himself falling for Liz. He asked her out a number of times. She turned him down, saying she had other plans. "Maybe another time," Liz would say. Rob was puzzled. They had been spending a lot of time together. They would have lunch, walk to classes, and share very personal thoughts and feelings. Rob had come to think Liz felt the same way he did. Now he began to question that.

Why is this girl being like this? he wondered. *Is she just leading me on?*

After a few months, Liz told Rob she was seeing someone. Rob was disappointed. But at least he finally understood her behaviour. He didn't see much of Liz for several months. He felt he had been honest about his feelings for her, but she hadn't been honest with him. (Liz later told Rob the other relationship wasn't as deep and serious as theirs, and she realized she had hurt him.)

After some time, Rob began hearing from Liz again. They resumed their friendship. Rob realized once again the very strong feelings he had for Liz. He hoped that by sharing more of himself, he would convince Liz he was the one for her.

Their friendship soon blossomed into love; by mid-1989, Rob and Liz were a committed couple.

They were both students and didn't have much money, so they spent their time simply. Saturday night was usually date night. They would go for walks in the park and see movies at the theatre. They spent a lot of time hanging out at Liz's house. They chatted and watched movies they rented. Rob would drop in to see Liz at her part-time job at a group home for the developmentally disabled.

Rob was impressed with Liz's gentle, caring nature. It showed in the work she did at the group home, and in the concern she had for others. "Liz had a way of making you feel that you were the most important person in the world to her," Rob said. "She really seemed interested in what you had to say."

At the same time Liz was also very quiet and very private. She had few close friends. Although she was beautiful, smart, and talented, she did not talk much about herself. She did not brag or go on about her talents. For instance, she was a skilled pianist who had spent years studying music. But for some time, Rob didn't even know she played piano. One day, Rob and Liz were hanging out in the family room at her house. Rob noticed a number of her certificates, proudly displayed by her parents.

"I was like, 'Whoa!'" Rob recalls. "'You never told me you play piano!'"

When Rob first heard Liz play, he was even more impressed. "I remember thinking to myself, you would have to have spent such a huge amount of time doing this to get to the level you're at. You'd think she would mention it," Rob said. "But she never did."

Rob knew that Liz was private. But he had never been very concerned about privacy growing up. "We had one telephone at home and it was in the kitchen," he said. "When I was on it, my mom pretty much knew who I was talking to and what it was about."

Rob didn't expect privacy at home. For some young

people, their bedroom is a private place where parents won't go without knocking. Not at Rob's house.

"My mom would just walk in whenever she wanted," he recalled.

Rob was the same way with his friends. He shared his feelings and thoughts about almost everything. "Liz was the opposite of me: my life was an open book, and hers was closed," Rob said. "There was almost an air of mystery about Liz."

Rob and Liz spent their time apart in very different ways. Rob met with his friends to play sports, catch movies, or just hang out. Liz would often stay at home by herself, writing in her diary or doing school work. Liz was very focused on her studies and strived for excellence.

"Liz was a perfectionist," Rob said. "I think a lot of people would look at her and say, she *is* perfect; she's beautiful, she's smart, really talented musically." Of course, no one is perfect. Rob came to think that Liz had difficulty admitting that: "Most of us accept the fact that we can't be perfect, even though we'd like to be. But I think for Liz it was just very difficult to accept anything else — in herself and maybe in other people, too."

One on one, Liz was a lot of fun to talk to. In a crowd, she preferred to watch and listen. She had very high standards for her friends, but wasn't critical of others. "She would never tell you to get lost — even if she wanted you to get lost," Rob said.

Rob and Liz got along well, rarely arguing. In fact, one of the only issues they ever fought about was Liz's use of herbal medicines. She felt they might help her with a food allergy. Rob was suspicious of the treatments and the doctors who recommended them. He begged Liz not to use them, especially when it was unclear what the side effects were.

It bothered Liz a lot when they argued. For instance, one night as they were getting ready to go out, Rob and Liz had a small disagreement. It grew into an argument. Rob spoke to Liz harshly. "You know, I think we'd better forget about tonight. I'll talk to you in a few days," he said, bringing the evening to a sudden end. For Rob, the fight was minor. But Liz was very upset and left crying. That night, Liz wrote in her diary that it was the end of their relationship. She was heartbroken.

"She had convinced herself our relationship was over — that I had dropped her that night and that's why I didn't want to see her the next day," Rob said. "The argument wasn't even really on my radar screen. But for her it was an absolute catastrophe."

Sometimes Rob could only guess what was going on

in Liz's mind. He was shocked when, one day in 1990, she showed up with bandages on her wrists. It looked like she had cut herself. Liz didn't want to discuss it. She said things were okay.

The hint that Liz might hurt herself was very troubling to Rob. Over time he had become aware of a dark side to his beautiful, gentle girlfriend. Liz could be unsure of herself. She became depressed and had thoughts of harming herself. Rob felt the best thing to do was give Liz love and support. He hoped that by being positive, he could help her see how great life could be.

As time went on, the bond between the two strengthened. Both Rob and Liz began to think of getting married. Liz had hopes for a happy, normal life. But she was troubled by doubts about herself and others. She filled her diary with these feelings, pouring her heart out on its pages. Liz even wrote about wanting to die. And she wrote much about Rob, including the doubts she had about their relationship. Liz dreamed about marrying Rob and having children. But she also thought about breaking up with him.

"*If I am so happy why do I try to talk myself out of breaking up with him every other night?*" a diary entry read. "*Why do I cry so much?*"

Liz's feelings ranged from being sure she had met her

future husband to angry outbursts about him.

"*I want to marry Rob and have two children,*" one entry read. "*This is the feeling I have waited for all my life. To be able to love someone unconditionally. I want to be the happiest me . . . I was born to love this guy.*"

Yet, there were entries that seemed to have been written by a confused and troubled young woman.

"*Life sucks and it's getting worse by the day,*" Liz wrote in the final pages of her diary. "*I hate my job, I hate school and Rob is becoming a pest. Last night I wanted to put a bullet through Rob's head and everybody that was bothering me.*"

In some entries Liz appeared to be deeply depressed. "*Every morning when I rise I try to think of a reason why I shouldn't kill myself . . . I want death to come and end . . . this pathetic life that is getting worse by the day.*"

When Rob became aware of Liz's diary, he was shocked by some of the entries. He had assumed he would marry Liz and spend his life with her.

"I thought we had a real connection," Rob said. "Looking back now, I realize I was wrong."

CHAPTER THREE

MISSING

"Hey. That looks like Liz's car."

Rob was driving along Kingston Road in east Toronto, on his way to the gym for a workout. It was 6:45 p.m. on June 19, 1990, when he spotted a Toyota Tercel in a parking lot near the Scarborough campus. It was unusual that Liz's car would be parked there, near the wooded ravine that bordered the campus.

Rob pulled in to have a look. The Tercel was the only car in the lot. As Rob got close, he saw a Canadian Automobile Association sticker on the car that convinced him it was Liz's. The unlocked car was empty and no one was around. It was parked quite far from the building where Liz had a class at 7 p.m. Rob wondered what Liz could be up to; she had told him she planned to spend the day studying. Rob checked the nearby tennis courts. Liz wasn't there. He went back to the car and waited to see if she'd show up. *Maybe she's just out for a walk*, he thought. But the minutes ticked away and Rob remained alone with the car. Finally, at 7:10 p.m., he decided to head to the gym.

But his mind remained on Liz. Rob had been wondering about some of the things that had been happening. The previous week, at a picnic dinner with a client from Liz's group home, Liz suddenly said she was skipping her evening class. Later in the evening they were watching a movie at Liz's house when she got a phone call. She said very little, responding with just yes or no. After the call, she said she had to take her client back to the group home, which was only a few minutes away. Liz was gone for nearly an hour. Rob couldn't help but wonder if Liz had gone to meet someone. But he did not question her about it. Now, after finding Liz's car, the incident came back to him.

Maybe it has something to do with what happened the other night, Rob thought. *Maybe she's there to meet somebody.*

After his workout, Rob went to the building where Liz's evening class took place. He waited as students filed out. Liz was nowhere to be seen. As he watched, Rob saw a nice-looking young man who also seemed to be waiting for someone. He couldn't help but wonder again: *Is that guy waiting for Liz?*

He felt a bit silly, but he wanted to know. So Rob waited, staying out of sight in case the young man was there to meet Liz. But a girl came out and they walked away arm in arm. The last of the students exited the class and there was still no sign of Liz.

Rob went back to the parking lot. Liz's car was gone.

Okay, Rob said to himself. *This is getting really weird.*

Rob was getting worried. He went to the Bains' house and talked to Liz's mom, Julita.

"Liz wasn't at her class tonight and I can't find her anywhere," he told Mrs. Bain. "Have you heard from her?"

Mrs. Bain stared silently at Rob for a moment. "I thought she was with you," she said finally.

Both of them felt a hint of alarm. It wasn't like Liz to drop out of sight. Rob headed back to the U of T campus to have a look around. He called a friend who was in the class Liz was supposed to be at that evening.

"Did you see Liz at class tonight?" Rob asked.

"No," the friend replied. "She didn't show up."

Rob hung up. *What the heck is going on?* he wondered.

Rob hung around the campus. He joined in a pickup volleyball game with some friends. At about 11 p.m. he went home, where he told his mom about finding Liz's car. Right away, Mrs. Baltovich became worried. Rob found himself trying to calm her. "I'm sure everything's fine," he said. "She's probably just at a friend's house or something. Liz told me that she might be getting together for dinner with her friend Arlene."

Rob decided to call Liz's house once more. The line was busy. He called Liz's brother and left a message about the evening's strange events. Late in the evening, Rob went to bed in his basement room. He left his mom a note for Liz in case she called: "*Tell her I was worried,*" the note said. "*And tell her I'll see her tomorrow.*"

Early the next morning, the phone at Rob's house rang. It was Liz's mom.

"She didn't come home last night," Mrs. Bain told Rob. "We haven't heard from her. We don't know where she is, Rob."

Rob felt a shock run through his body. "I'll be right there," he said.

Rob tried to remain calm as he spoke to Liz's mom. She was clearly worried and he didn't want to make her any more anxious. But he couldn't prevent the rising sense of panic he felt. *Something is seriously wrong here*, he thought.

And then the chaos began.

Rob rushed to Liz's house. He found Mrs. Bain obviously concerned. But she tried to keep calm as the other members of Liz's family searched their minds for anything that might explain where Liz was. Rob again mentioned Liz telling him that she had planned to get together with Arlene.

The mood brightened somewhat.

Rob drove to Arlene's house.

"We haven't heard from Liz and she said you guys might get together last night," Rob said.

"No, Rob," Arlene replied. "I never saw Liz yesterday."

Rob's heart fell. The hope he felt vanished.

Mrs. Bain phoned the Toronto police to report Liz missing. Meanwhile, Liz's loved ones turned their rising panic to action. They split up and searched the streets of Scarborough for any sign of Liz. Rob went to the Rouge Valley parking lot where he'd seen Liz's Tercel. There was no sign of Liz or her car, and no clue as to what might have happened. A dejected Rob returned to the Bain home. Liz's family had found her diary. Entries showed she was depressed, and maybe even thinking about suicide. Rob's mind flashed to a few weeks before when Liz had turned up with her wrists bandaged.

And for the first time he heard the things that Liz had been writing about him. He read of her love for him. But he also read about her frustration with their relationship. He learned of the rage she sometimes felt toward him.

"She said some pretty nasty things about me; she said she wanted to put a bullet in my head," Rob remembers.

The very last entry in Liz's diary was the most alarming: "*Everybody can rot in hell!*" Liz had written, underlining the word "hell."

Liz had filled the pages with raw emotions, her anger and doubts. This was a different Liz from the woman that Rob and her family knew and loved.

"Reading her diary was such a shock," Rob said. "We all felt like, 'Who is this person writing these things?' Because it was so unlike her.

"I remember thinking, who is the real Liz here? Is it the Liz I see two or three times a week, or is it this person writing in this diary? Or is it somewhere in between?"

All morning, Rob couldn't help but think that someone might have harmed Liz. Reading the diary, he now wondered if she had hurt herself. Or maybe she had just gotten so fed up with things she decided to take off for a while. He shared this thought with Liz's family. Everyone tried to remain hopeful. But the hours crept by and still nobody knew where Liz was.

Liz just needs to sort things out, they told themselves. *Soon she'll be home, safe and sound.* "For the better part of the next two days that was what we thought," Rob said.

Rob and Liz's family kept up their search. Posters of

Liz and her car were handed out, asking anyone with information to help. The police sent information about Liz and her car to other forces. The tension grew. Hours crawled by. Rob clung to the hope that Liz was okay. But two days passed without a sign of either her or her car.

If we don't have the car and we don't have Liz, then Liz is out there somewhere driving the car, he thought, trying to remain hopeful. *Whenever we find the car, we'll find her.*

4

CHAPTER FOUR

A TERRIBLE DISCOVERY

On the afternoon of Friday, June 22, 1990, Liz's car was found. It was parked outside an auto repair shop near her Scarborough home. The Toyota was empty. But inside, police made a terrible discovery. In the back seat they found a pool of blood.

The news was crushing for Liz's loved ones.

The blood in the car meant something terrible had happened to Liz. But there were clues that someone else had driven it. The car had been backed into the parking space, something Liz likely would not have done. And there was a tape in the player that might not have belonged to Liz. Police also found a pack of cigarettes, although Liz didn't smoke very often.

The alarming find changed the nature of the case. "When they found the car and she wasn't in the car or anywhere near the car, that's when we started thinking,

'Okay, we're back to foul play,'" Rob said. "It went from being a missing person case to a homicide." Detectives Steve Reesor and Brian Raybould of the Toronto Police Homicide Squad took over the case. They began by closely questioning Rob, and Liz's family. They wanted to find out what Liz had been doing before she'd gone missing. They wanted to know what might have been going through her mind. On June 24, a tired and frantic Rob called the detectives: "I'm beginning to think that maybe it's murder," he told them.

That evening, Rob gave the first of many statements to the police. He said over and again that he was trying to help find his missing girlfriend. But the police were suspicious.

Why is this guy talking so much? they wondered. *Is he trying to put us off the trail? What does he really know about what happened here?*

The search for Elizabeth Bain resumed. It went on into the summer. Volunteers searched forests, creeks, and other sites in the Toronto region. Police searched the wooded area where Rob had seen Liz's car the day she went missing. On July 11, Liz's twenty-third birthday, her parents Julita and Ricardo held a press conference. They begged whoever had taken Liz to return her to her family or tell the police where her body was hidden.

"Please," an emotional Mrs. Bain said. "We just want to bring our daughter home."

The press was full of stories about the terrifying mystery: *Where is Elizabeth Bain?* they asked.

The police worked steadily. They interviewed potential witnesses. And as the case moved ahead, they kept their prime suspect firmly in their sights: Robert Baltovich.

• • •

As they took over the case, Detectives Reesor and Raybould focused on Rob. Just over an hour after Liz's car was found, they had applied for permission from the courts to have Rob watched closely. The police believed that Rob would lead them to Liz's body. The police then expanded their efforts. They bugged Rob's phone and his car. They listened as he talked to his family and friends.

From the point of view of the police, it made sense to take a close look at Rob. When trying to solve a murder, officers start by examining the people closest to the victim. Then they expand their focus outward. Victims usually know their killers. Often there are deep connections between them. So the boyfriend of a young, beautiful woman would be a logical suspect. As far as anyone knew, Liz didn't live a lifestyle that would bring her into contact with dangerous people. So it made sense that the killer was someone close to her.

There's no doubt that Liz's diary gave Detectives Reesor and Raybould reason to suspect Rob. What if Liz had told Rob she wanted to break up and he became angry? Was it possible he had decided that if he couldn't have Liz, no one could?

The police concluded that Rob killed Liz in a rage. They thought he hid her body near the Scarborough campus, likely in the heavily forested ravine. They believed he moved it when the investigation heated up. Later, they thought that Rob had driven Liz's body to the area of Port Perry, northeast of Toronto. Rob knew the area, as he had worked there as a camp counsellor in his teens. It is an area of forests, farmers' fields, and wetlands. It is a place where a body could be well concealed.

Rob doesn't fault the police for investigating him. "I was her boyfriend," he said. "I was the person they would have thought was the most likely to have been responsible."

Yet to this day, he believes police had a chance to catch the real killer. But they let it slip away as they spent weeks and months gathering evidence against him. "They had a chance to take a step back and say, 'let's take a look at what we have and can we really be sure this is the guy?' And I think that window closed. I think the die was cast," he said.

Rob doesn't think the police targeted an innocent man on purpose. But he feels their focus on him kept them from looking at other suspects. "I really believe that from the first moment, the police had decided in their minds not only that I was a suspect, but that I was the person who committed the crime. I wouldn't say my fate was sealed, but I would say the course of the investigation was pretty much set in motion," he said. "They took all of their resources and they're all directed to Rob Baltovich to the exclusion of anyone else."

The police had formed an opinion of Rob and the way in which Liz had been killed. But that doesn't mean they were right. Problems between two people can be seen from the outside as more sinister than they are. Rob thinks that police saw tension between him and Liz as a reason for him to have caused her harm. Although it was wrong, the idea that Rob was a jealous and violent boyfriend became central to the police case.

The police felt they knew who killed Liz. All they had to do now was prove it.

5

CHAPTER FIVE

"WE THINK YOU DID IT."

As the search for Liz went on, Rob was often in contact with the police. He shared with them his thoughts and fears about what might have happened. He told them he was worried that she was depressed. He was afraid she might have hurt herself. Rob also told them about the time he'd found her with her wrists bandaged. On Sunday, June 24, five days after Liz went missing, he gave police a lengthy statement.

The police didn't believe that Rob was an innocent person trying to help them. His cooperation made them suspect him even more. They wondered if he was trying to cover up his role in Liz's disappearance. They thought maybe he was trying to send them in the wrong direction. Some of the things Rob said convinced the police of this. For instance, on July 5, a little over two weeks after Liz went missing, Rob took a lie-detector test. As he was chatting with Detective Frank Wozniack before the test began, he made what would become known as the "homicidal thoughts" statement. It would be used as evidence against him later.

A transcript of the conversation shows the officer asked Rob if he'd ever thought about harming Liz:

Officer: Don't get me wrong but have you ever thought about maybe harming Liz in any way? Ever thought about . . .

Rob: Yes, yes I have.

Officer: Is that right?

Rob: Yes.

Officer: What comes to mind?

Rob: That was, um, in the wake of being I guess rejected by her, like I guess it would be in the fall of '87.

Officer: Okay, I'm not suggesting you're the type of guy who would do something like this . . .

Rob: Oh, that's okay.

Officer: Have you ever thought about killing her?

Rob: Yes.

Officer: When was that?

Rob: That was the fall of '87.

Officer: Well if you thought about it, how did . . . how would you have planned it out?

Rob told the officer he'd never actually planned to hurt or kill Liz. He explained that after he got to know her in 1987, he became very fond of her. He wanted to date her. But her reluctance to go out with him had hurt him.

Rob: I became convinced in my heart that there was no one more right for her than me and no one more right for me than her . . . and the enormous depression that I felt after being rejected by her . . . plunged me very deep into despair.

He quickly told the officer that during the time he was dating Liz, he'd never thought of hurting her. He added that he had respect for the law, and the job the police do.

Rob: This is going to sound corny to you, but I believe very strongly in our legal system and I really truly believe that if you do something wrong somewhere along the line you're going to get caught.

Why would someone make such comments to police officers? Rob was answering honestly: back when Liz had turned him down, he had been hurt. He had wished he could hurt Liz's feelings the way she had hurt his.

"It was a momentary wish to lash out against someone who had hurt me," Rob said later. "Someone who appeared to have done so deliberately. It wasn't the fact Liz had rejected me so much. It was that she knew about my feelings for her and pretended not to know. And she never told me she was seeing someone else."

Rob felt the fact he was willing to take the lie-detector test would clear him as a suspect. He had nothing to hide. He thought that if he helped police cross him off their list, they could move on to find the real suspect. And he thought that answering "no" to the question might convince the police he was trying to cover up negative feelings he had toward Liz. But Rob was already under suspicion. His words had the opposite effect. The police believed they had even more proof that Rob was jealous and had harmed her.

Rob realizes that talking to the police helped support their belief that he was behind whatever happened to Liz. But he was trying to help the police find Liz or find out what had happened to her.

"Liz was my girlfriend. I felt like I knew Liz better than anyone. At that time I felt I was in the best position to tell them what they needed to know about Liz in order to figure out what happened to her. I felt I had to speak to them. Because if I didn't, they would not have the information they needed," Rob said. "In the beginning it just seemed logical to me they'd want to talk to me."

Rob was in an interview room at the police station. Detective Reesor confronted him with the stunning accusation. "Rob," he said, looking straight into the young man's face, "we think you know what happened to Liz."

Rob's mind began to race. *Oh my God*, he thought. He felt the beginnings of sickness in his stomach. *These guys actually think I did it.*

His heart was beating fast. *Where did this come from?* Rob wondered, staring at the detective. *This can't be happening.*

In spite of the shock and alarm he felt, Rob tried to remain calm. The detective described their theory of how he had killed Liz and disposed of her body.

"We know Liz was trying to break up with you," Detective Reesor said.

"No," Rob tried to interrupt.

"And we know you couldn't let her go," the officer continued. "And, Rob, that's when you killed her."

"No, that didn't happen," Rob stammered.

"You killed that girl and you hid her body."

"No . . . no."

"And then you moved her. And only you know where Liz is."

"No," Rob said, "you're wrong about that. No. That didn't happen."

The detective pressed on. Rob felt panic rising. No matter what he said, the police had decided he was a killer. He had not been charged or placed under arrest. But he knew they were determined to prove their case. They would be putting all of their resources into doing so. He realized Detectives Reesor and Raybould felt sure they had their man.

"It was almost like, is this really happening?" he said. "It almost seemed like I was in a dream."

6

CHAPTER SIX

THE POLICE BUILD THEIR CASE

Of course, the police were not relying just on Rob's statements to build their case against him. They spent weeks and months talking to witnesses. Some people told them they had seen Liz with Rob the day she disappeared. Some said they'd seen the couple arguing in the days before it.

Liz's sister Cathy told police she'd overheard an argument between the two on June 18. Rob denies this. Vanessa Sherman, who worked at the group home with Liz, said she'd seen Liz arguing with a man she said was Rob. She said Liz and Rob were outside the home, talking and gesturing. As Liz turned and walked away, Rob "gave her the finger" and squealed away in his car. Sherman said Liz seemed upset when she came in.

"What's up with you and Rob?" Sherman remembered asking.

"I'd rather not talk about it," was Liz's response.

Rob denies the fight ever took place. Vanessa Sherman had never met him. She didn't tell the police about the supposed argument until well after Rob had been arrested. Much later, Rob's lawyers contacted Ms. Sherman as they prepared to appeal his guilty verdict. At that point, she claimed to remember nothing of the incident.

A woman who lived near the Scarborough campus, Suzanne Nadon, contacted police after Liz's disappearance. She told them she had been awakened in the early morning hours of June 18 by the sounds of a man and woman arguing. She said a car drove off and she watched as a girl walked alone along the road. When Nadon saw posters with pictures of Liz and her car, she believed the young woman she saw was Liz. This was evidence from someone who didn't know either Rob or Liz. And this witness came forward after Rob had been identified as a suspect.

Other witnesses provided much more damaging evidence against Rob.

Marianne Perz was working in June 1990 as an instructor at the Scarborough College Tennis Club. She had known Liz for about ten years, but had never met Rob. When she learned on June 23 that Liz was missing, she contacted the police. She said she had seen Liz on Tuesday, June 19, between 5:30 and 6:15 p.m. She was sitting at a picnic table near the tennis courts. Perz recalled that Liz was with a group of people, including a man she didn't recognize. After Perz saw Rob's photo in the newspaper on July 1, she gave another statement to police. This time Perz said she remembered she had seen Liz at exactly 5:40 p.m. When police showed her Rob in a photo lineup, she said, "That's the man Liz was with."

In early July, David Dibben contacted police. He told them he had seen a man driving Liz's car early on the morning of Friday, June 22 (the day Liz's car was found in Scarborough). This was near the town of Port Perry, about an hour northeast of Toronto. Dibben described the man as being in his mid-twenties with blond hair, a receding hairline, and a moustache on his thin face. Dibben said he and the driver were stopped at a red light. They briefly looked at one another before the light changed and they moved on. His description of the suspect didn't resemble Rob. Even so, Mr. Dibben picked Rob out of a photo lineup the police showed him.

Police had a few witnesses hypnotized, including Perz and Nadon. This was supposed to help them with their memories. Police wanted a more detailed description of the man they said was with Liz the day she went missing. Under hypnosis, the witnesses gave details that convinced police Rob was their prime suspect.

Rob was upset by the rising suspicion, which did not end with the police. Months after his daughter went missing, Liz's father told a reporter he knew who had harmed her.

Rob said, "Before I was arrested he [Liz's father] came out in a newspaper article that was published by the *Toronto Sun*. He was quoted as saying, 'I know who murdered my daughter.'" Bain went on to say he hoped the person would have the decency to tell Liz's family where she was. Rob wasn't named in the story, but he knew Bain was referring to him. Even before that, Liz's mom had confronted Rob.

"We know you did something to her," she said. "We want you to tell us where Liz is."

The words filled Rob with dread. He had always gotten along very well with Liz's mom. He had never imagined she would suspect him of something so terrible.

If I've lost Mrs. Bain, he thought, *then I'm in trouble.*

All this time, the media said Rob was the prime suspect. Some reporters claimed that because he was Liz's boyfriend, he was the person most likely to hurt Liz. But everything that was reported came from sources other than Rob. Rob did not speak to the reporters, though some tried hard to get him to talk.

In one instance, a reporter from the *Toronto Sun* confronted Rob at his house.

"There are some questions about your relationship with Liz," the reporter said. "Some people think you may know what happened to her."

"It's too bad people are talking like that," Rob replied. "But really, I can't give you any comment. The investigation is still going on. Sorry."

Just then, Rob noticed movement behind a white van parked near the end of his driveway. A *Sun* photographer popped out and began snapping pictures of Rob. Shocked, Rob withdrew into the house.

"You have no ethics," he told the reporter before shutting the door behind him.

A short while later, the phone rang. It was the reporter. "Do you still think I don't have any ethics?" she asked.

"No comment," said Rob, hanging up.

7

CHAPTER SEVEN

UNDER ARREST

It was hard for Rob to live under the cloud of suspicion. But he tried to carry on as best he could. He went to work each day, facing questions from friends who told him they'd been contacted by police.

"I got a call from the police and they interviewed me," one guy said to Rob. "They're telling me about this terrible thing you've done. What's going on?"

It frustrated Rob. Some people he had considered friends began to avoid him. *Why?* Rob asked over and again. *Why do they think I did this?*

As the summer of 1990 gave way to autumn, it seemed to Rob as if the police activity surrounding him became less intense. He hated the idea of being a suspect. But he believed that whatever happened was beyond his control. "Because nothing had happened for two months, you start thinking well, if it hasn't happened yet, maybe it won't happen," he said. But the police were still gathering evidence. Finally, the detectives decided they had enough proof to act.

On the morning of November 19, 1990, as Rob prepared to go to work, Toronto police arrived at his home and arrested him. They charged him with first-degree murder, the most serious offence in Canada's Criminal Code. Police laid the charge even though they did not have Liz's body. To this day, no trace of her has ever been found. It had been exactly five months since Liz had gone missing.

For Rob, the arrest was a stunning event. Still, he had known for months police considered him their prime suspect.

"It was a shock, but it didn't come out of the blue," he said. "In my mind I always knew there was a possibility it would happen."

Rob was handcuffed and placed in a police car. News cameras surrounded the vehicle, capturing images of Rob in the back seat. But Rob didn't try to hide his face. He held his head high, staring straight ahead. Later, the *Toronto Sun* ran a large picture of Rob on the front page, describing him as looking relaxed. The message was clear: only a guilty man could remain so calm when arrested for such a horrible crime.

But what was going through Rob's mind at that moment was the opposite: *I am innocent*, he thought. *I have no reason to hide my face in shame.*

In a way, Rob saw his arrest as his opportunity to prove his innocence. *Maybe now all the nonsense is over,* he thought. *It's time now to show I didn't do this and I'm innocent. Maybe now there's a finish line.*

That's not to say Rob didn't realize how serious his situation was. If he had any doubt, the news photographers surrounding the police car reminded him of that.

My life is never going to be the same again, Rob thought.

• • •

Rob was held at the Metro East Detention Centre, a Toronto jail. He was placed in protective custody. Authorities do this when they feel an inmate might be harmed by others or may even harm himself. It meant spending twenty-four hours a day in his cell.

Soon after his arrest Rob appeared in court for a bail hearing, He became aware of the huge amount of time and effort the police had put into building the case against him. Rob felt a rising sense of alarm as he heard details of the evidence against him.

Oh my God, he thought. *For the last five months they've been doing nothing but planning on arresting me.*

The carefully presented evidence — and the realization that so many people were sure he had murdered Liz — crushed Rob. When he was denied his release on bail, it was like a blow to the head.

If I'm denied bail, that means this judge actually believes they have a case, he thought. *That means I'm going to be here for a while.*

As hard as it was, Rob realized he had to remain strong. He couldn't despair, even though it was hard not to. But the stress of being trapped in jail, the dread of what might await him, and the frustration at being falsely accused got the better of him. One day, early in 1991, after staying locked up through Christmas, he was on the verge of a breakdown. He called his mom and poured out his heart. His voice cracked and tears flowed down his face.

"Mom," Rob sobbed, "I'm really scared. I don't know what's going to happen. What if I'm convicted, Mom? What if I never get out of here?"

Rob's mom listened as he expressed his fears. She did her best to try to tell him that everything would be all right.

"We believe in you and we love you," Mrs. Baltovich said as she tried to soothe her son. "And we'll always be here for you."

As the conversation wound down, Rob began to feel a sense of relief. He had kept his emotions pent up since his arrest. The phone call was a good release. His fears flooded out of him. As he said goodbye, he began to feel a peace he hadn't been able to imagine since his arrest.

You know what? he said to himself, *it doesn't matter what happens at this point. I'm going to be okay. I'm prepared now — even for the worst.*

"It was almost like there's this incredible storm, and then it passes and you see this nice rainbow," Rob recalled years later. "It was the lowest moment I'd had since the whole process began."

After his bail was denied, Rob learned his next court appearance was months away. He vowed to remain strong. He would prepare for the fight to declare his innocence.

Rob Baltovich wouldn't taste freedom again for 354 days.

8

CHAPTER EIGHT

ROB'S CASE GOES TO COURT

Rob stayed in jail, waiting for his case to be heard in court. The first step was a preliminary hearing in 1991. *Preliminary hearings* are held in cases involving serious charges, including first-degree murder. A lower-court judge hears the case against the accused. Then the judge rules whether or not there is enough evidence for the charges to go to trial in a higher court. Rob's case was heard first in Ontario Court in Toronto by Justice Ted Ormston.

During his bail hearing, Rob had already heard much of the case the Crown outlined. But at the preliminary hearing he actually heard it from the mouths of the Crown witnesses, including David Dibben, Marianne Perz, and others. Rob's defence lawyers, William Gatward and Michael Engel, were allowed to cross-examine the Crown witnesses. They tried to raise doubt about their evidence.

When Justice Ormston made his ruling, part of it went in Rob's favour. The judge ruled that the case against Rob would go to trial, but the charge was reduced to second-degree murder. The difference between the charges is important. Canada's Criminal Code describes first-degree murder as a killing committed on purpose and *premeditated*, which means the killer planned the murder. Second-degree murder is a lesser crime, but still a very serious one that is dealt with harshly. The Crown must prove the accused committed an act he or she knew would likely lead to the death of the victim. In second-degree murder, the suspect is accused of acting without pre-planning — for instance, in a moment of extreme anger or rage. The Crown might be able to prove Rob killed Liz when he was very angry. But they did not have grounds to prove he had planned to harm her.

First-degree murder is the most serious crime. A conviction brings an automatic life sentence. There is no chance for the prisoner to be released on *parole* until he or she has served twenty-five years in prison. The penalty for second-degree murder is also an automatic life sentence. But the judge can set *parole eligibility* — the number of years a prisoner must serve before he or she can apply to be released from jail under terms set by the

National Parole Board. The prisoner may still have to remain in jail anywhere from ten to twenty-five years. It is still a life sentence. Even after the prisoner is released, he or she remains under control of the authorities. The prisoner can be sent back to jail if parole rules are broken or another crime is committed.

The reduced charge gave Rob's lawyers hope that he might be released on bail. Rob waited in a provincial jail for the ruling. He had tried to keep his spirits up. But being in jail was wearing him down. He began to fear that he would be convicted of killing Liz, even though he was innocent.

Maybe I'm just kidding myself, he found himself thinking during the long hours in jail. *Maybe it doesn't matter that I'm innocent. Maybe I'm going to be in prison for the rest of my life.*

Rob was sitting on his bed in his cell, listening to the news on the radio, when he heard his name. He sat up, his heart thudding, and listened closely.

"A judge has ruled that Robert Baltovich, facing a murder charge in the disappearance of his girlfriend, Elizabeth Bain, will be freed on bail until his trial," the reporter announced.

Rob sat silent, letting the news sink in. *Oh my God,* he thought. *I'm getting out of here. I'm getting out of jail.* A tingle ran up his spine. It was the first good news he had heard in months.

"To this day, as crazy as it sounds, that was the happiest day of my life," Rob said later. "Because being in jail really breaks you down physically and emotionally. When it came over the radio I almost fainted, I was so happy. I almost started to cry."

Out on bail after almost a year in jail, Rob tried to live as normal a life as he could. He had some freedom, but still had to observe strict rules. He had to live with his parents. He could not leave the house at certain times. If he broke those rules, his bail would be cancelled and he'd be right back in jail.

Rob took his partial freedom as a sign that finally things might go his way. But serious challenges lay ahead. Rob faced a trial where a jury would be told he was guilty of a horrible crime. They would be told that he deserved to be sent to jail for life.

9

CHAPTER NINE

THE TRIAL BEGINS

The trial of Rob Baltovich began in the Superior Court building on University Avenue in downtown Toronto in February of 1992. The trial was the subject of intense interest. The courtroom was filled with reporters and spectators. They were all eager to hear details of a crime that had shocked the city.

Rob was surprised to see the crowded courtroom benches. They were filled with reporters staring at him and scribbling in their notebooks. "Wow," he whispered to his lawyer, "are all these people here to see me?" Rob's mind raced. *This is serious*, he said to himself. *The whole city's watching.*

Rob was represented by Toronto defence lawyers William Gatward and Michael Engel. When Rob realized he was a suspect, a member of Rob's family suggested Mr. Gatward as a lawyer. Rob hired Gatward and, as the case proceeded, Engel joined the defence team. The men had represented Rob at the preliminary hearing where his charge was reduced to second-degree murder. So when the trial date arrived, he stuck with them.

As the trial began, Rob was *arraigned*. That means the charge against him was read out in court. Rob entered a plea of not guilty. Then the lawyers for the Crown and defence chose twelve jurors from a group of people ordered to appear for jury duty. A jury is chosen from a large group of people. This is so that the accused person is judged by citizens much like him — his peers. The lawyers finally agreed on a jury of four women and eight men.

Journalist Thomas Claridge was assigned to cover the case for *The Globe and Mail* newspaper. He remembers there was great interest in the case. Everyone wanted to know about Liz's disappearance and Rob's arrest and trial.

"The media had given very wide coverage. Anytime you have the disappearance of a beautiful young Toronto-area woman, the media's going to be interested," Claridge said. "It had all the elements of a murder mystery."

Claridge remembers that it was no surprise the police had focused on Rob. The idea that Liz Bain had been killed by a jealous boyfriend made sense. "You always look for the husband or the boyfriend. There was nothing surprising about that," Claridge said. "And right up to the time of the trial there was no other suspect."

Jurors began hearing evidence on February 4, 1992. Many witnesses were called to the stand as prosecutor John McMahon presented the Crown's case against Rob. It is the *prosecutor's* job to convince jurors — to make them believe beyond a reasonable doubt — that the accused is guilty of the charge before the court.

Among those McMahon called to the witness stand were two people who linked Rob to Liz's disappearance. Marianne Perz, the tennis coach, had told police she'd seen Liz with Rob at the Scarborough campus the day Liz went missing. David Dibben testified he saw Rob driving Liz's car near Port Perry soon after her disappearance.

These witnesses were important to the Crown's theory of the murder. Jurors were told that Rob was jealous and angry that Liz no longer wanted to be with him. They heard that he killed her in a park near the university campus, hid her body and went to the gym. The Crown believed that, when Rob learned police suspected him, he retrieved Liz's body, put it in her car and drove to the Port Perry area. He hid the body there before returning to Toronto. Then he left the car at the auto body shop.

McMahon asked Perz if the man she had seen Liz with back in 1990 was in court. She pointed at Rob. "That's him," she said. "His hair is much shorter, he's thinner and more pale."

All eyes in the courtroom shifted to Rob. He sat silent, unable to protest.

Perz and Dibben were not perfect witnesses. Questioned by Rob's lawyer, Perz admitted that at Rob's preliminary hearing she had said she wasn't one hundred per cent sure he was the man she'd seen with Liz.

"There must still exist a doubt in your mind that the man you saw was Robert Baltovich," Engel said.

"Yes," Perz agreed.

Jurors also heard Dibben's original description of the man he saw driving Liz's car: blond and having facial hair. The description didn't match Rob's appearance.

The jurors looked on silently. Some of them scribbled notes. Rob found himself wondering: *What's going through their minds? Who do they believe?*

McMahon wasn't finished. The Crown called Michael Fraser, a jail guard. Fraser testified about a conversation he had had with Rob in November of 1990, soon after Rob was arrested. He said Rob had told him the police didn't have much of a case against him.

"I said, 'What if they find the body?'" Fraser testified.

"He said there will be no chance of that."

Fraser admitted he didn't know if Rob was hinting he had hidden the body. Rob might have meant he had helped in the searches for Liz and felt she would never be found. But the message the Crown was sending was clear: Rob was sure he had hidden Liz's body so well it would never be found.

The Crown also called police officers to testify about statements Rob had made. They included Frank Wozniack, the lie-detector officer. He had heard Rob admit to thinking about harming Liz as far back as 1987, when she turned him down for a date. And jurors heard from Suzanne Nadon, the woman who recalled seeing Liz having a late-night argument with a man near her home.

Eric Genuis had dated Liz before she went out with Rob. He told the court that Liz had told him she wanted to end her relationship with Rob. "She said leaving Rob was the right thing to do," Genuis said.

The jury also heard from Liz herself. The Crown said Liz's diary proved her relationship with Rob was far from perfect. The prosecution argued Liz was confused and upset about Rob. The diary showed her desire to leave him.

"Why do I keep thinking about breaking up with this guy?

I don't want to be with him for the rest of my life," read one page. "*Or do I?*"

Even as she described how well Rob treated her, Liz wrote in her diary, "*Leave him. He has destroyed you. Get out while you have something left.*

"*This nice guy is truly a wolf in sheep's clothing,*" the jury heard Liz say through her diary.

"*Beware!*"

The jurors listened intently. Their faces showed nothing. But Rob was very much aware of the message the Crown was sending them. They were hearing that Liz was very unhappy and wanted to leave, but Rob wouldn't let her. Rob knew it was far from the truth. But he could only sit in silence. He wondered what impact the passages were having on the people who would decide his fate.

Rob at 21, with a friend (not Elizabeth Bain).

Smoke shop owned by Rob's dad, where Rob used to work as teen. (Toronto, ON)

Rob in the prison library at Warkworth Institution.

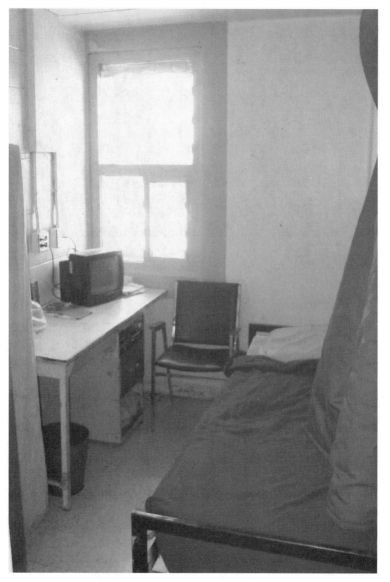

Prison cell at Warkworth penitentiary, similar to what Rob would have lived in.

A sign outside Rob's Scarborough home on March 31, 2000, the day he was released on bail. It reads: "After 8 yrs of injustice, Rob's free."

Rob and his father on the day he was ordered released on bail by the Ontario Court of Appeal. Friends and family gathered for a celebration of Rob's release after eight years in jail.

Paul Bernardo on the day he was arrested in February 1993.

Rob in 2009.

10

CHAPTER TEN

CRACKS IN THE CASE

As he watched the case unfold, *Globe and Mail* reporter Thomas Claridge began to feel more and more strongly that an innocent man was being tried for murder. He was troubled by what he saw as serious cracks in the Crown case. These included the timing of events surrounding Liz's murder.

He heard that blood found in Liz's car, days after she went missing, was still wet. He began to question the idea that she had been killed days earlier. For the Crown's theory to be correct, Rob would have had to kill Liz three days before the car was found. But if that was the case, how could the blood in the car still be wet? *No*, Claridge thought, *Liz was killed much closer to the time the car was found. And by that time, Rob was helping to search for her and giving statements to the police. So how could he have done it?*

"There was just no possibility of Rob having done it," Claridge said.

Some of the testimony heard by jurors contradicted the Crown's theory of Liz's killing. For instance, Ruth Collins was the owner of a health food store who knew Liz as a customer at her shop. She said she saw Liz in a car on Kingston Road in east Toronto at about 8:30 p.m. on June 19, 1990. This was a couple of hours after the Crown said Liz had been killed. John Elliot, another man who had come forward to offer information to police, said he had seen Liz's car near Port Perry the day after she disappeared. But the Crown believed Rob had driven the car out of Toronto after that date. And the Crown said Rob had parked Liz's car at the auto body shop on the Friday morning it was discovered. But a woman who worked at the shop said she had seen it there early on the Wednesday morning after Liz went missing.

Watching from the public gallery, Claridge saw two Rob Baltoviches. One was the polite, mild-mannered man who showed up each day at court. The other was the jealous, scheming killer described by the Crown.

"There was very little evidence to support it," Claridge said of the picture of Rob as a cold-blooded killer. "That was simply a Crown theory."

Claridge was also troubled that some key witnesses

had been hypnotized. He thought police were trying to mould the evidence so that it supported the case against Rob. (Much later, higher courts would agree. Evidence gathered from witnesses who have been hypnotized is no longer allowed in trials in Canada.)

Prosecutor McMahon admitted from the outset the case against Rob was *circumstantial*. That means there was evidence that could mean he was guilty, but that he had no direct proof, such as an eyewitness to the crime. McMahon made the most of the evidence he had, Claridge recalls. In the face of such a tough case, Rob's lawyers seemed outmatched. McMahon, a skilled prosecutor, was able to make a weak case into a strong one.

Rob's lawyers argued he wasn't at the university at the time the murder was said to have happened. They also pointed to the possibility that someone else might have killed Liz. And they said that, since no body had been found, no one could say for sure Liz was murdered.

But Claridge was amazed and dismayed when Rob wasn't called to the stand to testify. He thought the jurors should hear Rob's defence in his own words. Otherwise, how could they find him anything but guilty? Claridge wondered if the jurors might be thinking, *If I was charged with murder and I was innocent, I would be up there saying I was innocent. So he must be guilty.*

"As things went on, I didn't see justice being done," Claridge said.

Rob also felt that he should testify. He wanted to tell his side of the story. He, too, felt the jurors might get the wrong message if he remained silent. But his lawyers reminded him he had already spoken at length to the police. They told him that testifying would do him no good. McMahon was very skilled at cross-examining witnesses, Rob's lawyers warned him. "You've given statements," they told Rob. "There's nothing you can say in court that you haven't already said."

As the trial went on, Rob saw himself being described as a jealous, angry man who would commit murder to keep his girlfriend from leaving him. It wasn't true, but there was nothing he could do about it.

"I felt like I was listening to somebody else being described. It was so far from the person I am," Rob said. "It's the most sickening feeling in the world. You feel like if you react angrily it's going to be seen in a negative light. But if you don't react and if you remain silent, not showing any emotion, you will be seen in a bad light as well."

Sitting in the courtroom, Rob had a weird feeling. *This trial isn't even about me anymore,* he thought. *It doesn't matter what I say, it doesn't matter what I do. In the end it's really up to those twelve people to make what they will out of all this.*

Convincing the jury that Rob was a jealous boyfriend who had been dumped by Liz was a key part of McMahon's case. He called witnesses like Liz's friend, Nancy Sicchia. She testified Liz had told her she wanted to break up with Rob.

"The big problem with their relationship was jealousy," she said. "She told me Rob was quite possessive and a pretty jealous man. She hated it."

And Stephen Annett, who was dating Liz's sister when Liz went missing, said Rob was worried about Liz.

"He asked me if I thought Liz was seeing someone behind his back," Annett said as jurors listened. "Liz was the best thing he had ever found, and he wouldn't want to let her go."

In his final speech to the jury, McMahon once again accused Rob of killing Liz when she tried to leave him.

"I leave you with the words Elizabeth Bain wrote in her diary: *'Please, God, give me the courage to leave him,'*" McMahon said. "On June 19, 1990, Elizabeth Bain had the courage to leave. She paid the ultimate price." McMahon looked each juror in the eyes as he pressed home his argument.

"She paid with her life."

11

CHAPTER ELEVEN

THE VERDICT

Before jurors consider their verdict, they are addressed by the judge. These final words are called a *charge to the jury*. In this address, the judge reviews the evidence heard during the trial. He or she advises the jury on how they might use the evidence as they seek the truth. As Rob listened to the judge in his case — Superior Court Justice John O'Driscoll — he found himself becoming deeply worried that the case against him was being stressed as the truth. Justice O'Driscoll said Liz probably hadn't harmed herself. The judge also urged the jury to carefully consider evidence that Rob was in Liz's car near Port Perry after she went missing.

"If Robert Baltovich is the driver of the car, where is he coming from at that hour in that car?" the judge asked as jurors listened. "What was he returning from doing?"

Listening to the charge, Rob felt rising alarm. *He's*

just repeating the Crown's case! he realized. *If you're sitting on the fence, who are you going to go with? Are you going to go with the judge, or this guy who the police think did it?*

Following the charge, jurors were *sequestered*. They were shut off from the outside world — no TV, no phones, no radio. They had no contact with anyone but the other jurors. No one knew what they discussed or which way they might be leaning. For Rob and his family, the tension grew as each hour passed. After a day and a half, word arrived that they had reached a verdict. When he realized his fate was about to be announced, Rob gathered his family around him.

"Listen," he said, looking into his mom's worried face. "We don't know what the decision is going to be. But I want you to know whatever it is, I'm going to be okay."

Rob's lawyer tried to help Rob be hopeful. "Don't worry," he said, a tight smile on his face. "You'll be sipping lemonade tonight."

There is little in real life that is more dramatic than a crowded courtroom awaiting a jury's verdict. The air is as hushed as in a church. But it is almost as if an electric current is running through it. Everyone knows that something huge and important is about to occur. It is an event that will be life-altering for those involved. Rob watched the jurors file in; none glanced his way. When the judge asked the jurors if they had reached a verdict, the foreman stood up.

"We have, Your Honour."

"What say you?" the court clerk asked.

Rob's throat tightened. This was the moment he had been waiting for for years.

"Guilty," came the response.

A gasp rang out in the courtroom. Rob's mom broke down crying. Rob glanced over his shoulder to where some of his friends sat. He saw their faces blank with shock. Some of them were crying. Rob's own mind was blank.

"I had already prepared myself for the worst, so I didn't really have much reaction," he said. "I couldn't believe it."

Journalism student Marnie Luke was in the court-room when the verdict was announced. She described Rob's reaction in *The Ryersonian* newspaper:

> *He bit his bottom lip, bowed his head for just a few seconds, and then regained the same confident composure he has maintained throughout the trial. Moments later, he was stripped of the few remaining symbols of his identity. His tie was removed, two good luck charms were*

*taken from the breast pocket of his navy suit
jacket, and from his pants pocket, five dimes
were confiscated.*

It was March 31, 1992. The judge ordered Rob to be held in custody until a sentencing hearing in May. As he was led away, Rob winked at a reporter he had befriended during his ordeal. The wink said that, in spite of the verdict, he would remain strong.

"Take care," he said to her.

• • •

Following the guilty verdict, Rob's parents were in disbelief.

"What happened?" Rob's dad asked the defence lawyers.

"How can they find him guilty when he didn't even do it?" his crying mom asked.

Speaking to reporters after the verdict, Liz's parents said they were sure of Rob's guilt. Liz's mom Julita said that the family's pain went on, especially as her daughter was still missing.

"Until we find our daughter's body, we will never be at peace," she said, her face a picture of grief.

The media printed strong reactions to the verdict. *The Globe and Mail* published an article questioning the fairness of the trial and the verdict. The day after the verdict, a *Toronto Sun* headline read, "*Elizabeth Bain's prince was a jealous monster.*"

On May 1, 1992, Rob's sentencing hearing was held. The crime carried an automatic life sentence. What was left for Justice O'Driscoll to rule on was the number of years Rob would serve in prison before he could apply for parole. When asked if he had anything to say to the court, Rob rose.

"I would like to say I had absolutely nothing to do with Liz's disappearance, and I am totally innocent of this crime for which I have been convicted," he said. "That is all."

Then it was Justice O'Driscoll's turn. The judge left no doubt about his feelings for Rob. "In cold blood you killed your girlfriend," he said. "Your acts from day one are as reprehensible as one can imagine . . . you have high intelligence, but you are absolutely devoid of heart or conscience."

The judge then uttered a phrase that would be remembered by many who heard it: "You are right to expect justice," he said. "But you have no claim to mercy."

Justice O'Driscoll then announced that Rob would be imprisoned for at least seventeen years.

12

CHAPTER TWELVE

PRISON

Seventeen years.

Over seventeen years, a child will pass through infancy into childhood. The child will enter primary school and eventually graduate from high school. That child will grow, passing the many milestones we use to measure time and life: getting a driver's licence, graduations, and celebrations. Seventeen birthdays. Seventeen Christmases.

Justice O'Driscoll had ruled. Rob would serve at least seventeen years in prison before he could apply for parole. The judgment also meant he would live with his sentence and criminal record for the rest of his days.

Rob was being moved from a provincial jail to a federal prison, where inmates serving long sentences are kept. It was a scary prospect. "The key now is surviving," Rob realized. "I don't want to die in prison."

He'd heard many things about prison, but wasn't sure what to believe. He began asking around, talking to guys who had been in prison before. Rob wanted to know what to expect and how to handle himself. His fellow prisoners tried to help. They told him what could lead to trouble.

"Don't gamble," one guy told him.

"Never borrow money," another said.

"Stay out of other people's arguments," another inmate advised.

And every one agreed on one key point: "Mind your own business."

Rob was sent first to Milhaven Penitentiary, a large, high-security prison near Kingston, Ontario. It holds convicts serving sentences for serious crimes. Milhaven is also the first place new federal prisoners are taken. There, officials decide where inmates should serve their sentences — in high-, medium-, or low-security facilities. Milhaven is a place often filled with tension. Men there are either at the start of long sentences or have been inmates for years. They can become hardened and angry.

Prison was the last place Rob had ever thought he'd end up. And, even though he had spent a lot of time behind bars after his arrest, prison was a foreign and frightening place. Rob was a middle-class kid from Scarborough. He had grown up living as normal a life as you could imagine. Nothing had prepared him for the grim routine of prison. On one of his first days at Milhaven, Rob was taken out of his cell. He was led, along with other prisoners, to the cafeteria for dinner. Earlier, there had been trouble near Rob's cell. Guards had used tear gas to put a stop to the incident.

Rob held a cloth over his mouth as he made his way to the cafeteria, the bitter stench of tear gas thick in the air.

Is this really happening? he wondered.

Although the days ahead seemed terrifying, Rob did his best to keep up his spirits. He tried to stay focused on his hopes for an *appeal* of his conviction. Appeals are reviews of cases for errors that might have led to unfair trials and incorrect outcomes. Rob's only hope of avoiding a long prison term was for the Ontario Court of Appeal to rule in his favour. The appeal court reviews cases heard in lower courts, including the Superior Court, in which Rob's trial had been held. Appeal judges must decide if mistakes were made in those courts. Sometimes it is ruled that the original trial was conducted properly. In that case, verdicts and sentences are upheld. Sometimes appeal court judges find that errors have been made. If those errors resulted in an unjust verdict or an unfair trial, a new trial might be declared necessary.

Rob came to view his time in jail as a temporary stop on the way to proving his innocence. As long as his appeal was a possibility, there was hope.

I'm not going to be a lifer, Rob told himself. He realized that without hope, his chances were slim.

I'm not that old, he thought. *I've got my books, and I've got my family and friends. I may have to be here two, maybe even three years. I still have a long life ahead of me. I still have a lot going for me.*

And, he told himself over and over again, *I am innocent.*

Rob was held at Milhaven for nine months before being moved to Warkworth Institution. He would spend the rest of his sentence in Warkworth, in the countryside near Peterborough, Ontario. In a way, leaving the tense, grim setting of Milhaven for the new prison was a relief for Rob.

Set in a long, low valley amid acres of farmland, Warkworth is a large prison that holds hundreds of inmates. Prisoners live in cell blocks that are arranged around a central yard with intersecting walkways. If you didn't know you were in a prison, the yard might look like a town square to you. Warkworth has manufacturing shops where prisoners can work during the days.

It also has a large gym and a library. Inmates live in small cells — not much bigger than the bathroom in an average home. Each cell has a metal cot, and a table and chair. When inmates are placed in their cells, a large metal door swings shut on them.

People are always moving around in prison. It's rare for a person to find a way just to be alone. The buildings are made of brick and metal with tile floors. Sounds echo all the time. Lighting is cold and harsh.

Several buildings lie outside of the cell block area. Some are workshops and classrooms. One large, single-storey building, set off to the side, contains cells for solitary confinement. Inmates can wind up in "the hole" for fighting or breaking prison rules.

The entire prison — cell blocks, workshops, guard towers — is surrounded by a high fence. The fence is topped by rolls of coiled razor wire. The message of the fence is clear: Don't even think about trying to get out of here.

In the fall of 1992, Rob's lawyers began an appeal of his conviction. They also applied to have Rob released on bail until his appeal was heard. But bail was not granted. Rob would remain imprisoned until his appeal.

Despite all the negatives, Rob felt hopeful when he looked around at his new home. Some people who have spent time in jail will tell you that it is a very boring place. There is a set routine in which little changes. One day blends into the next; time becomes a blur. But Rob had always been active. He enjoyed reading and studying. He was determined to make the most of his time in jail. He read an enormous amount and worked in the prison library. He worked out in the gym. He also tutored inmates who were trying to earn school credits.

"I was able to keep my body healthy; I was able keep my mind healthy," he said. "Prison can be very boring. But if you can create a world for yourself, it goes a long way in getting you through it."

Rob quickly learned that the way to survive prison was to keep himself fit and optimistic, and to respect others.

"You'd be amazed. Please and thank you really count," Rob said. "A lot of guys are in prison because people didn't say please and thank you to them, or mistreated them. Sometimes it's not the person who starts the fight that gets arrested; it's the person who ends it."

As he talked to people and made friends, Rob found the way he felt about the law was changing. So was his attitude toward people who got into trouble. Before, he had been sure that criminals should be harshly punished. He had agreed with the idea of the death penalty for the worst offenders, even though capital punishment was abolished in Canada in 1976. But being convicted and sentenced for a crime he didn't commit changed his way of thinking. A lot had to do with what he learned from his fellow prisoners.

"I met a lot of really smart people in prison. I met a lot of people that had really sad lives. A lot of people think that anyone who's in prison has brought about their own bad luck. But that's not the case at all," Rob said. "Many people live lives of real hardship. And prison woke me up to the fact that my life wasn't as bad as I thought."

Looking around, Rob saw that he was much more fortunate than many of his fellow inmates. *I have an education. I have a family that cares about me,* Rob realized. *A lot of these guys have nothing.*

But time in prison is hard time. As the months and years dragged by, sometimes Rob struggled to keep his spirits up. Five years passed. Life on the outside went on. It was hard not to feel forgotten and lonely.

Rob didn't know it, but he and his case hadn't been totally forgotten. There was a growing feeling, especially in the media, that he had been wrongly convicted. In 1995, Rob sat down for interviews with Derek Finkle, a journalist who believed in Rob's innocence. In 1998,

Finkle published a book. The title, *No Claim to Mercy,* was drawn from the harsh words used by Justice O'Driscoll when he sentenced Rob. The book created more debate about Rob's case.

The years dragged on. Rob's appeal still had not been heard. At times, he felt his resolve slipping. All he could do was wait.

13

CHAPTER THIRTEEN

A TRAGEDY AT HOME

In August of 1997, five years after his conviction, Rob suffered a terrible loss. His seventy-year-old mother, Adele, died after a battle with lung cancer.

When he first learned about her illness, Rob tried to be calm. He tried to reassure his mom. One time, shortly before she was to have surgery, she visited him. Rob was comforted that she looked well.

"The treatment's going okay," his mom told him. "And I'm cutting down on my smoking."

Rob smiled at his mom. In spite of her illness, she was in good spirits. He felt much better.

After his mom had her surgery, Rob kept in touch with his brother by phone. At first, things seemed to be going well. But one day, Rob heard tension in his brother's voice.

"Rob," he heard his brother say, "Mom's slipping."

Rob felt alarmed and helpless. He had to get to his mom. But he was trapped behind prison walls. "I was freaking out," he said. "I didn't know what to do."

Rob quickly applied for a temporary release from prison so that he could visit his mother. At first, authorities said he wasn't eligible. He had seen his mom at the prison just a short while ago. But as the seriousness of her illness became clear, parole officials changed their minds. They started working on a release for Rob. Their decision came too late.

"She died that day or the day after," Rob said. "It was pretty brutal. Definitely my worst day; way worse than being convicted. I just went to my cell and bawled my eyes out. I couldn't believe it; it was just such a shock."

During his time in prison, Rob had spoken on the phone with his mom regularly. It was more to reassure her than for himself. "I talked to her at least every other day. It was more important for her," he said. "I knew if I wasn't in contact with her she would worry.

"When I first got convicted I was worried how she'd deal with it," Rob said. "She stayed really strong for me. She told me, 'You've got a lot of people out here who support you one hundred per cent and you've got to do whatever you have to do to stay strong.'"

A heartbroken Rob applied for release to go to

his mom's funeral. He was almost denied because of a mistake on his record. His file said he had broken his bail rules before his trial and he'd been sent back to jail, which wasn't true. The error was corrected. A few days later, Rob left Warkworth in the company of two corrections officials.

For the first time in years, Rob stepped beyond the fence that surrounds Warkworth. For the first time in years, he was on the outside of the prison, looking in. Rob rode in a car along the long driveway that leads from Warkworth up to a country road. The car turned west. Looking back, Rob saw the prison. It was a group of drab buildings, towers, and razor wire set at the bottom of a long, gently-sloping plain. Around the prison for miles there was little but cornfields, cows, and farmhouses. To the west was the tiny village of Warkworth. Far to the south lay the grey, cold waters of Lake Ontario.

For Rob, it was a bittersweet day. He was as close to freedom as he had been in years. Yet he was crushed by the loss of his mom. The guards — Rob still remembers them as "good guys" — treated him with kindness. They drove him to Toronto, even allowing him a brief tour of the hometown he'd been taken away from so long ago.

"I was basically free for the whole day. They let me go by my house and by my dad's store," he recalled. "It was a weird day; you couldn't pick a worse day to get out of prison than to attend your mother's funeral. But at the same time you're out and you get to see all these people you haven't seen in a long time. It was kind of an overwhelming thing."

In a way, the death of Rob's mom robbed him of a dream. He had long imagined walking out of prison to see her smiling face. Now he realized that hug he had waited for years to give her would never happen.

If I ever get out of this place, my mother's not going to get a chance to see it, he realized. He was as sad as he'd ever been in his life.

After the funeral, Rob was taken back to Warkworth. Once again, he was just another prisoner.

Robert Baltovich spent eight years in prison, waiting for the day he'd have the chance to prove his innocence. He and his lawyers would have to convince a panel of judges that an injustice had been done in his case. "Everything I did in the eight years I was in the federal system was basically preparing myself for when I got out," Rob said.

To get out, he would need the support and expertise of one man. This man has earned a reputation in Canada for fighting on behalf of the wrongfully convicted. Rob's fate would rest with Toronto lawyer James Lockyer.

14

JAMES LOCKYER

Rob's only hope of setting the record straight and getting out of prison was to have a great lawyer fighting on his behalf.

I can't help myself. My family and friends can't help me, Rob realized. *The only one who can really help me is my lawyer.*

He decided to approach James Lockyer. He hoped the famous lawyer would agree to represent him.

Born in 1949, James Lockyer was raised and educated in England. While studying law in university, he became interested in social issues. He got involved during the 1960s in the movement against the racist government of South Africa. Lockyer came to Canada in 1972 and taught law at the University of Windsor in Ontario. He remained socially active, organizing demonstrations and protests to help various causes.

In 1980, he formed a law firm in Toronto. The firm quickly became known as a hard-working and effective team. They often fought the police and the legal system in court. Lockyer found his true calling in the appeal courts. There, he represented people who had been wrongly convicted. Over the years he has fought dozens of appeals, including those of Guy Paul Morin and David Milgaard. Both these men were convicted of murders they did not commit.

Lockyer joined with other lawyers to form the Association in Defence of the Wrongly Convicted (AIDWYC). This organization's sole focus was fighting for innocent people convicted of crimes.

Lockyer believes that the justice system is slanted more toward convicting people than to finding out the truth. He also feels that a lawyer makes the biggest impact during his or her career by fighting appeals. He believes those cases bring about real change in the system.

When Lockyer met Rob Baltovich at Warkworth in early 1999, he felt he was looking into the eyes of an innocent man.

"Rob," he said, "I believe in this case. And I believe in you. I'll do everything I can to get you out of here."

Lockyer joined Rob's legal team. His first order of business was to apply to have his client released on bail.

It would be no small task. People convicted of murder very rarely get bail. Rob had been refused bail in 1993 when he filed an appeal. At first, Lockyer was doubtful about his chances. But as he reviewed Rob's case, he felt more confident. In March 2000, almost eight years after the end of the murder trial, Lockyer went to the Court of Appeal to argue for Rob's release.

The passage of time had not reduced interest in Rob's case. His bail hearing attracted many reporters and observers. Attending were people like Rubin "Hurricane" Carter, who himself had been wrongly convicted of murder. Carter had been imprisoned for twenty years before being proven innocent. "Hurricane" had been a successful boxer before being sent to prison. He was now a leading spokesman for the wrongly convicted and worked with AIDWYC.

"I'm here because Mr. Baltovich is a client of the Association in Defence of the Wrongly Convicted, and AIDWYC feels very strongly that he is innocent and should not be in prison," the outspoken Carter told a crush of reporters outside Osgoode Hall, the Toronto courthouse where appeals are heard.

Inside the courthouse, Lockyer argued that new information had emerged since Rob's 1992 conviction. He told the judges the case for an appeal was strong.

He said that there were real concerns about the verdict in the trial.

To the delight of Rob and his lawyers, the judges agreed. On March 31, 2000, the eighth anniversary of Rob's conviction, they freed Rob on bail until his appeal. Even the judges noted how unusual it was for someone facing a murder charge to be granted bail. But they said the court had to recognize cases as strong as Rob's.

The judges made note of many of the arguments put forth by Lockyer. They called the police case against Rob "wholly circumstantial," which means that there was no direct evidence proving him to be the killer. The judges ordered that Rob was to live in Toronto with his dad, Jim.

Rob almost couldn't believe what he was hearing. After all his years of anguish, he was being released from prison.

It was a beautiful, sunny, early-spring day when Rob stepped out the front door of the downtown Toronto building. He was surrounded by reporters and cameras. They all asked, "How do you feel?"

Rob paused for a moment. The reporters waited.

"It's a great feeling," he finally said. "Jail isn't a pleasant place."

It was all Rob would allow himself to say. He had been warned by Lockyer and the other lawyers on his team not to brag or gloat about the decision.

Rob walked out of the courthouse and into the sunny afternoon as cameras followed him. He savoured the moment and the feeling that finally things might be starting to go his way.

"I honestly believed when I stepped out of prison that I was never going back," Rob said. "I was that confident."

Rob's family was overjoyed about the ruling. Rob returned to a house decorated with cheerful yellow ribbons. Derek Finkle, who had written a book raising questions about the case against Rob, was there. He wrote an article describing the happy occasion. Rob had been locked up for eight years as society and technology progressed. That day he sent his first e-mail and had his first conversation on a cell phone. And he ate his first takeout hamburger in nearly a decade. It was the best-tasting burger ever.

Later that evening Rob gathered with family and friends for a big feast of Chinese food. He was sitting in his home, surrounded by loved ones, still trying to believe he was free.

"Hey, Rob," someone said. "Don't forget your fortune cookie!"

Rob looked at the cookie in his hand. "I'm scared to open it on a day like this," he said. Everyone around him laughed. They looked on as Rob drew a breath, cracked open the cookie, and unfolded the tiny slip of paper. The words swam before his eyes.

"Success and happiness will be yours," the fortune said.

15

CHAPTER FIFTEEN

BUILDING A NEW CASE

Finally freed from prison after eight long years, Rob
tried his best to resume a normal life. He graduated
from the library sciences course at Seneca College. He
got a job at the Royal Ontario Museum in Toronto. And
he returned to university to earn a Master's degree. "My
life pretty much got as back to normal as you could
imagine," Rob said.

Although he was finally out of prison, Rob wasn't
completely free. Conditions of his bail were that he had
to live with his father in Scarborough. He also had to
remain in Ontario and report to police every two weeks.
Rob was also ordered to keep a job. A curfew kept him
at home between midnight and 5 a.m. each day.

In addition to working and studying, Rob spent time
at the offices of his lawyers, keeping tabs on how his
appeal was going. He learned that, in reviewing the files

on the case, Lockyer had found evidence that the jury at Rob's first trial had not heard. This evidence would be put forth when Rob's day of appeal arrived. Lockyer had found "a mountain of information," Rob said.

Police never revealed evidence of a witness who saw Rob on the Scarborough campus the night Liz went missing. The jury at Rob's trial heard that Rob had already killed Liz by that time, so there was no reason for him to be there. But Naz Tonbazian, who knew Rob from the weight room, said he saw Rob outside Liz's classroom that night.

Lockyer also looked into the statement by Liz's sister. She said she overheard an argument between Rob and Liz just before Liz went missing. But the evidence showed she originally told police it was several days before that. This raised questions about the reliability of her evidence.

The Crown also told the jury that Rob had killed Liz on June 19 and hidden her body in Colonel Danforth Park. They said he moved her early on the morning of June 22 when he became aware police planned to search the area. But police had actually searched the area on June 21 and hadn't found any sign of Liz. This cast doubt on the Crown's theory that Rob had moved Liz after killing her.

At the first trial, jurors heard that shortly before she went missing, Liz had written a *"Dear John" letter*, breaking up with Rob. They heard the letter disappeared when police began investigating Rob. Lockyer found the letter — a page from Liz's diary that she gave to Rob — in the Crown's files. It did not say that Liz wanted to break up with Rob. Instead, it explained that she had turned him down for dates because she had a boyfriend when they'd first met. Discovery of the letter weakened the Crown's theory that Liz had planned to break up with Rob.

When the date for Rob's appeal finally came in September 2004, Rob felt confident his lawyers had built a strong case. It was time for the appeal court judges to rule in the case of Robert Baltovich.

Rob's legal team took centre stage at Osgoode Hall. They presented their arguments and the "fresh" evidence uncovered after the original trial. The lawyers also focused on the charge Justice O'Driscoll had delivered to the jury in 1992. They argued that the judge's comments made the trial unfair because he had urged the jury to reject Rob's defence.

Rob's lawyers suggested that Elizabeth Bain had been taken and killed by someone else. At the time of Rob's trial, his defence team had no other suspect to point to. But by the time of his appeal, the case of Paul Bernardo was well known. Paul Bernardo had been sentenced to life in prison for abducting and killing two young girls.

Police learned he had been committing crimes against women in Scarborough at the time Liz went missing. In fact, Paul Bernardo had admitted to being the man who for years had been known as the Scarborough Rapist.

On December 2, 2004, the Court of Appeal judges made their ruling on Rob's case. They declared that Rob had not received a fair trial. They set aside the guilty verdict. The judges ruled that Rob ought to have another trial.

In their long, written ruling, the judges listed a number of reasons for their decision. They wrote about the fresh evidence and the possibility that Paul Bernardo might have been the man who killed Liz. The judges also took a close look at Justice O'Driscoll's role. The judge, they ruled, had tipped the scales against Rob in his charge to the jury. They wrote that he had supported the prosecution's case while tearing down the defence.

"The charge to the jury was unfair and unbalanced," the judges concluded. "The appellant's conviction for second-degree murder must accordingly be set aside."

Rob's defence team had won the day. They began preparing for a new trial. They got ready to argue Rob's innocence and urge jurors to focus on another potential killer. That man, they intended to argue, was Paul Bernardo.

16

CHAPTER SIXTEEN

PAUL BERNARDO

In June 1991, fourteen-year-old Leslie Mahaffy disappeared from outside her home in St. Catharines. Almost a year later, in April 1992, fifteen-year-old Kristen French also went missing. She was forced into a car as she walked through a church parking lot. Both girls were later found murdered.

Their killer was Paul Bernardo. He was arrested in 1993 after his wife, Karla Homolka, gave police information about those abductions and murders. She also told police about the assault and killing of her own sister, Tammy. Tammy's death at Christmas in 1990 had been ruled accidental, but was later found to have been murder.

The spotlight on Paul Bernardo led to talk that he was responsible for many more violent crimes against women, including Elizabeth Bain's murder. Police learned Paul

Bernardo was the Scarborough Rapist, who first came to their attention in May 1987. Bernardo established a reign of terror in the area. He eventually confessed to fourteen attacks on women between 1987 and 1990.

On September 1, 1995, Paul Bernardo was found guilty of first-degree murder in the deaths of Kristen French and Leslie Mahaffy. He was automatically sentenced to life in prison with no possibility of parole for twenty-five years. But he received an even heavier sentence when the courts declared him a dangerous offender. He was considered highly likely to harm someone else if he were ever to be released. It is possible Bernardo may never be freed.

• • •

Lawyers arguing Rob's case before the Ontario Court of Appeal suggested the crime might have been committed by Paul Bernardo. They said police focused on Rob so strongly that other suspects were not considered.

Some journalists accepted the theory as well. In an article published in April 2008, *Toronto Star* reporters Betsy Powell and Peter Small listed what they called a "powerful body of evidence" that points to Bernardo as the culprit:

Between March 1986 and May 26, 1990, Bernardo committed 21 sexual assaults in the

Scarborough area — 14 of which the Crown admits — with a pattern of escalating violence.

He attended U of T's Scarborough campus, from which Bain disappeared, and took his girlfriends to adjoining Colonel Danforth Park.

Receipts found in Bernardo's house in St. Catharines show he frequented various stores in, or near, the Scarborough area around the time of Bain's disappearance.

An ex-Bernardo girlfriend knew Bain and introduced her to Bernardo in the mid-'80s. The ex-girlfriend also had a crush on Bain's brother, which once caused Bernardo to fly into a jealous rage.

Bain was seen at a restaurant with a blond man (Paul Bernardo was blond at the time; Rob Baltovich was not) several weeks before her disappearance. The restaurant was one Bernardo was known to frequent. Around the same time she was seen arguing with a blond man in a red Jeep in a plaza [where] another Bernardo watering hole [was located].

At 5:30 p.m. on the day Bain went missing, a female U of T student saw a blond man on the Scarborough campus staring, frightening her as she made a phone booth call. She wrote a description of him and said he resembled a composite drawing of the Scarborough rapist.

A package of Du Maurier Light cigarettes — Bernardo's brand — was in the glove box of Bain's car.

Bain's car was found backed into its parking spot, consistent with how Bernardo parked.

The radio was tuned to CFNY 102.1, Bernardo's favourite station. A New Order recording, another favourite, was in the cassette deck.

It was also noted that David Dibben had told police the man he saw driving Liz's car near Port Perry was blond and had facial hair. That's a description that did not fit Rob. But it did match Paul Bernardo.

Not everyone bought into the Bernardo theory. *Toronto Star* columnist Rosie DiManno wrote that it was easy to blame Paul Bernardo for Liz's disappearance. She believed that there was a lack of proof linking him to the incident. In an April 2008 article entitled "*No proof in Bain's car to pin killing on Bernardo*," she wrote that no evidence had been produced to establish a link: "No trace of Paul Bernardo's DNA was ever found in Elizabeth Bain's car. There is simply no . . . evidence to support that position. The fact remains there is nothing connecting Bernardo to that car."

• • •

Bernardo talked with police in June 2007 at Kingston Penitentiary where he is serving his life sentence. He was asked if he killed Elizabeth Bain. The video of the interview could be found on numerous news websites after a judge ruled it should be released to the public. Asked if he killed Liz, Bernardo replies, "The answer to that is no."

"Did you have anything to do with her disappearance?" an officer asked.

"No," Bernardo said.

"Did you know Elizabeth Bain?"

"Not that I know of."

The officer asked, "Had you ever met her?" to which Bernardo responded, "I'm going to answer that one with 'I don't remember.' Because if I did, I don't remember."

It's not surprising that Paul Bernardo would deny

involvement in Liz's death. He has been found guilty of terrible crimes. But he still tries to portray himself in a positive light. In the same interview quoted above, he told police that Karla Homolka was not honest when she described the murders they were involved in. He tried to make himself look better.

He may have been clinging to the hope, however faint, that he might one day be released from prison. Admitting to any connection to Elizabeth Bain would not be helpful.

As well, what reason would he have to help prove Rob is innocent?

After all this time it's likely impossible to know if Paul Bernardo was responsible for what happened to Liz. But the fact remains that at the time Liz went missing, Paul Bernardo was attacking women in Scarborough. We know his crimes grew more serious. He is a convicted murderer.

His role remains one of the mysteries surrounding Liz's death.

17

CHAPTER SEVENTEEN

PROVEN INNOCENT

On April 22, 2008, Robert Baltovich once again stood before a jury. And, once again, the panel filed into the courtroom with a verdict. But this trial was far different from Rob's 1992 trial. This jury did not have to sit through a long trial and hear evidence. This jury had deliberated for only a few minutes before deciding.

Moments earlier, Crown prosecutor Phil Kotanen had risen to open the trial. Instead of presenting the Crown's case, he told the jury he had no case to put before them.

"I will not be making an opening," Kotanen said. "I will not be calling any evidence. I have no submissions to make except to invite an acquittal on a lack of evidence."

Jurors followed Kotanen's advice. Rob heard the words he had been waiting for years to hear.

"Not guilty," said the jury foreman.

Rob felt a rush of excitement. It was almost too much to believe. For the first time since his arrest in November 1990, he did not stand charged with the murder of Elizabeth Bain. He was no longer bound by the bail restrictions he had lived under since his release from prison in 2004. He was, for the first time in nearly two decades, a truly free man.

The outcome of the second trial wasn't a surprise for Rob. He and his legal team had learned of the Crown decision in the days before the trial began. Lawyer James Lockyer told a journalist he and his team were aware of weaknesses in the Crown's case. It was possible another trial might not be held. But the defence still had to work hard to be prepared, he said. He criticized the Crown for taking so long to admit it had no case.

"I had been expecting them to appreciate that their case had no substance and no merit years ago," Lockyer told the *Law Times*. "We finally get to the courtroom door and it's then that we finally get the right decision."

There was much debate about what might have led to the Crown's decision. Liz's dad blamed the outcome on delays in getting the case before the courts in a reasonable time. But Rob thinks it was that the Crown really had no case against him. "By electing to call no evidence, the Crown was saying 'we have no case,'" he said.

The outcome was what Rob had struggled for since being named as a suspect in his girlfriend's disappearance. He had finally, after all those years and legal proceedings, been declared not guilty of a horrible crime.

Of course, not everyone agreed with the outcome of the case. Liz's parents were bitterly disappointed that no one would be held responsible for their daughter's killing. They felt the police had charged the right man when they arrested Rob.

"We believe that he did it," Mrs. Bain told a *Toronto Star* journalist the day the acquittal came. "That doesn't change."

"I don't want [Rob] within ten feet of this house," Mrs. Bain said.

A few days later, the Bains repeated their belief in Rob's guilt. They felt the system had failed to bring to justice the person who had killed their daughter. And they were angry the Crown had decided not to hold a new trial based on evidence gathered by police in the early 1990s.

"The person convicted of her murder is allowed to walk free because the evidence can no longer be used," Mr. Bain said.

"This is not a verdict of innocence," Mr. Bain said. "This is a verdict of hands tied."

It's not just Liz's family who have doubts about Rob's innocence. *Toronto Star* journalist Rosie DiManno continued to closely follow the case over the years. She still believes the justice system got it wrong. In the fall of 2009, she said that Rob had caught a break. She claims the time between the investigation in the early 1990s and the new trial in 2008 made it impossible for the Crown to effectively pursue the case.

DiManno still believes Rob is the most likely suspect in Liz's death. "And I know few people who were around for the guilty verdict who feel any differently," she wrote in an e-mail. "However, there's no way to proceed with a new trial after all this time."

DiManno feels the public image of Rob Baltovich as a man who was falsely accused, convicted, and imprisoned is wrong.

"Do I think justice has been served?" she wrote. "Hardly."

Some writers changed their minds about Rob's guilt as his story unfolded. Others did not. Even journalists can react emotionally to terrible things, like a murder. For some people, the way Rob reacted proved he was guilty. He was calm and cool. Some felt he was cocky and arrogant. Those gut reactions can be hard — even impossible — to change.

Such doubts are to be expected, especially in a case like Rob's. He alone was identified as the suspect and even convicted. Although the verdict was the wrong one, it remains firmly in the memories of many. And some people accepted the picture of Rob as a jealous boyfriend who preyed on a vulnerable girl. Such beliefs, once they are established — especially in court, where the truth is supposed to reign supreme — are hard to erase.

Rob knows there remain doubts about his innocence. Much mystery continues to surround the case. But Rob says he tries not to let the doubts of others bother him.

"Their thoughts don't affect me," he says. "When it does affect me is when I feel it interferes with my ability to get a job, or to meet someone and settle down and have a family. It does hurt me."

18

CHAPTER EIGHTEEN

QUESTIONS LINGER

Rob's acquittal led to many questions about Canada's legal system. Some say there should be a pubic examination of what went wrong in Rob's case. Politicians such as MPP Peter Kormos agreed: "Robert Baltovich was the victim of a horrible miscarriage of justice. At the end of the day, the Crown had no evidence to offer up against him."

But Ontario's Ministry of the Attorney General ruled out an inquiry. Rob was disappointed with their decision. He had hoped an inquiry would reveal how an innocent man was convicted, while the true killer was never prosecuted.

"I wanted to get to the bottom of this case — find out what happened, where it went wrong, and find out a little bit more about who might have been responsible for Liz's disappearance," Rob said. "But I also wanted it from a very selfish point of view . . . I thought an inquiry would have really gone a long way in helping me prove my innocence.

"There is almost certainly other evidence out there," Rob said.

Sometimes when people have been wrongfully convicted, governments have paid them money. The payments are meant to admit a mistake has been made, and to compensate the person for the time they spent in prison. But in Rob's case, the Ontario government announced it wouldn't offer a payment. (The province did help Rob with his court costs through Legal Aid. This system assists people who are unable to pay the high costs of defending themselves. Rob estimated his legal bill at about $100,000.)

Attorney General Chris Bentley released a statement in January of 2010. He said that, although Rob Baltovich was acquitted, the police and prosecutors had acted properly in pursuing the case against him: "The Attorney General is convinced that, at every stage in this case, the Crown and police acted with integrity and in the best interests of the administration of justice." The announcement doesn't mean Rob will never be compensated for his ordeal. He has hired lawyers to sue the province of Ontario, the police, and others, including his original defence lawyers. The suit, which seeks $13 million, claims Rob was a victim of great injustice. The civil legal process is very complex, and may take some time to resolve.

"I know it's a long, drawn-out process," Rob said. "There is no right to compensation."

For now, Rob savours his freedom. But his experience has had a profound effect on his life. And he knows that his name remains forever connected to a high-profile crime that remains unsolved.

"After battling this thing for eighteen years and having it finally be over — at least at the moment — that's compensation enough. Just knowing that you can go home and you don't have to wake up the next day wondering when your next court date is," Rob said.

Rob is moving on with his life. He remains upbeat. He refuses to give in to anger or bitterness at what happened to him and toward the people who made it happen. "If I'm going to have a good life I can't spend the rest of my life hating and being filled with anger. Because then you end up not being the type of person people want to be around. I don't like being around negative people and I assume others feel the same way."

Rob realizes he can't change what has already occurred. And he points out that while many bad things happened once he was caught up in the justice system, some good came of his experience. He says he has grown and developed as a person. "I would definitely like to have lived my life without any of this happening. But I also know that you can never predict the direction your life is going to take. Even though my life could be better, it also could be much worse," Rob said. "It has given me a sense of perspective that I see lacking in many people. I wish I could somehow share some of what I've learned with them. But that's easier said than done, I suppose."

• • •

While Rob is committed to moving on with his life, questions about his case linger.

What if, from the time Liz went missing, police had focused on other potential suspects? Could more police resources have been used to look at suspects other than Rob?

How would the trial have turned out if jurors had not heard the final statement from Justice O'Driscoll? Remember that the Court of Appeal later ruled the statement had been unfair and tipped the scales against Rob.

What if Rob had testified? Would jurors have come to a different verdict if they'd heard his story in his own words?

The trial might have been fair if Rob's defence team had all the information they needed. This included witness statements and pages from Liz's diary that better explained the way she felt about Rob. Some of the evidence wasn't given to Rob's lawyers. Some of it was in police files that had not been requested by Rob's lawyers as they prepared for his first trial.

Also highly suspect was the use of hypnosis to help witnesses form better memories of what they thought they had seen. Did this help the witnesses to remember better, or did it make them "recall" things they had not seen?

And why didn't the Ontario government order an inquiry into the case? It might have revealed problems with the way the disappearance of Elizabeth Bain was investigated, and how the case against Rob was built. Whenever a wrongful conviction occurs — especially one in which an innocent man spends years in prison — such a review should be done. An inquiry might prevent it from happening again.

The most important question that lingers is this: Who killed Elizabeth Bain?

An innocent young woman was murdered. Will the killer ever be brought to justice? As long as the case remains unsolved, there is no justice for Liz, or for Rob either. Without another suspect, Rob remains the only person to be charged with the crime. He deserves to have his name completely cleared.

Until that question — Who killed Elizabeth Bain? — is answered once and for all, justice will not be served.

AFTERWORD

When I was preparing to meet Rob Baltovich as part of the research for this book, I found myself wondering just what he would be like. Rob wasn't hard to find. And he agreed right away to be interviewed. On the phone he was polite and friendly.

Still I wondered, what kind of person would Rob be? How would his experience have shaped him?

It's easy to imagine Rob would be bitter about what happened. I wondered if he would be suspicious of me, after having so many awful things written about him over the years.

Or maybe he would take the opportunity to complain about the justice system that had tried him and sent him to jail. Maybe his anger at others would get in the way of telling his story.

So it was a pleasant surprise to actually meet Rob.

To find out what he's like and to learn how his experience shaped him.

Rob is not an angry, bitter man. He is upbeat. He is peaceful. He is not consumed with anger. He is not obsessed with striking back at those who hurt him.

The way Rob explains his point of view is simple. Being angry won't change what happened. Bitterness does not help healing.

Rob has realized he has the rest of his life to live. He has chosen to be optimistic, not gloomy.

He has started a lawsuit, hoping the courts will order payment to him for his wrongful conviction. It's something that has happened in similar cases. A lawsuit is a way for Rob to be compensated. His life was interrupted and was never the same as it was before 1990. He lost the girl he loved. He's had trouble finding a good job. His life has been greatly affected.

Payment won't give Rob back the years he spent in prison. He could have been working and saving money if he hadn't been jailed. He could have been starting a family, enjoying his life, like the rest of us. A settlement may be a long way off, but it provides some hope that in a small way, things will be made right.

Rob still dreams of having a family, a good job, and the other things he wished for as a young man. He realizes the only way to achieve his goal is to be positive.

I learned a lot from Rob. He shows remarkable character. His story proves that as long as we hold onto our humanity — as long as we try to do right, and be good people — anything is possible.

ACKNOWLEDGEMENTS

Sincere thanks to Robert Baltovich, who throughout this project has been accessible, helpful, and encouraging. His willingness to assist and his openness in sharing his thoughts and feelings about his experience have proven invaluable.

Thanks also to Pam Hickman, who has been a patient and helpful editor. It has been a pleasure to work with Pam and her team throughout this project.

Peter Christie is a good friend and a fine writer who led me to this project.

And thanks, and much love, to my wife Pamela, who has been a constant source of encouragement and inspiration.

WHERE ARE THEY NOW?

STEVE REESOR, the homicide detective who investigated Robert Baltovich after the disappearance of Elizabeth Bain in 1990, rose to the rank of deputy chief of the Toronto police force in the mid-1990s. In January of 2005, he announced his retirement from policing to pursue a career in the private sector.

DETECTIVE BRIAN RAYBOULD eventually assumed command of the Toronto Police Homicide Squad. Under his leadership, the unit's rate for solving murders was an impressive seventy per cent.

JOHN McMAHON, the Crown attorney who successfully prosecuted Rob Baltovich's first trial in 1992, was appointed to the Ontario Superior Court as a judge.

JUSTICE JOHN O'DRISCOLL, who presided over the 1992 trial, has retired from the Superior Court bench.

JAMES LOCKYER continues to practice law in Toronto. He remains active with the Association in Defence of the Wrongly Convicted, fighting to correct injustice and free the wrongfully imprisoned.

ROBERT BALTOVICH lives and works in Toronto. He speaks publicly on issues of justice.

ELIZABETH BAIN was never found. The identity of her killer remains unknown.

TIMELINE

AUTUMN 1987 Robert Baltovich meets Elizabeth Bain at the Scarborough campus of the University of Toronto, where both are students. The two, who are in their early twenties, eventually begin dating.

JUNE 19, 1990 On his way to the campus gym for a workout, Rob finds Liz's empty car in a parking lot near the school. Liz is nowhere to be found. Although concerned, Rob continues on to the gym and later that evening speaks to Liz's mother Julita, who tells him she hasn't heard from Liz since earlier in the day.

JUNE 20, 1990 When Liz fails to come home during the night, her worried mother calls Toronto police. Rob joins members of Liz's family in a search for her.

JUNE 22, 1990 Liz's abandoned car is found near a Scarborough auto body shop. When police find blood in the car, the missing person case is upgraded to a potential homicide. During this time, Rob Baltovich gives statements to investigators who are beginning to see him as a likely suspect in Liz's disappearance.

NOVEMBER 19, 1990 Rob Baltovich is charged with the first-degree murder of Elizabeth Bain and taken into custody. He will remain in jail for nearly a year before being released on bail to await trial.

FEBRUARY 1992 Rob Baltovich's trial begins in Superior Court in Toronto. The charge has been reduced to second-degree murder after a preliminary hearing in a lower court. Jurors hear from prosecution and defence witnesses, but Rob himself does not testify.

MARCH 31, 1992 After a day and a half of deliberations, the jury returns with a guilty verdict. At a sentencing hearing a month later, Rob is sentenced to life in prison with no possibility of parole for seventeen years.

APRIL 1, 2000 After serving eight years, Rob is released from prison on bail as he awaits the hearing of his conviction appeal.

DECEMBER 2, 2004 Ruling his 1992 trial was unfair, the Ontario Court of Appeal orders a new trial for Rob Baltovich.

APRIL 22, 2008 When the day for the start of Rob's retrial arrives, the Crown announces it will be presenting no evidence and recommends the jury return a verdict of not guilty. After eighteen years, Rob Baltovich is finally cleared of the murder of Elizabeth Bain.

GLOSSARY

ACQUITTAL: the verdict when someone accused of a crime is found not guilty.

APPEAL: a request to review a case that has already been decided in court.

ARRAIGNMENT: a formal reading to inform a defendant of the charges against him or her. The defendant must then enter a plea — usually guilty or not guilty.

CHARGE TO THE JURY: when a judge instructs the jury about what law(s) to apply to the case and how to carry out its duties in deciding the verdict.

CIRCUMSTANTIAL EVIDENCE: evidence that does not directly connect someone to a crime, but places him or her at the scene or suggests they may have been involved. It cannot be accepted as proof unless all other explanations can be ruled out.

CONVICTION: the verdict when someone accused of a crime is found guilty.

"DEAR JOHN" LETTER: a letter written by a woman to her husband or boyfriend informing him that the relationship is over, usually written because she can't or is unwilling to tell him face to face. If it is written by a man to his wife or girlfriend, it is referred to as a "Dear Jane" letter.

DEFENDANT: the person who has been formally accused of and charged with committing a crime.

FIRST-DEGREE MURDER: the planned or deliberate killing of another human being.

PAROLE: the supervised release of a prisoner before the end of their sentence in prison. Parole often comes with conditions which, if violated, may result in a return to prison.

PRELIMINARY HEARING: a hearing held to decide if there is enough evidence for a trial. This is held after the accused has been charged with a crime.

PREMEDITATED: a murder is considered premeditated if the accused is proven to have thought about when or how to do it prior to the crime, in order to ensure success or to avoid being caught.

PROSECUTOR: the lawyer acting for the prosecution, usually the state (in Canada, the Crown). The prosecutor tries to prove the defendant is guilty.

SEQUESTERED: isolated from others. A judge may order that the jury be kept away from news, media, and other sources that might sway their decision. They must remain sequestered until the trial is over.

TESTIMONY: the statement of a witness under oath.

VERDICT: the decision of the jury at the end of a trial, usually guilty or not guilty.

FURTHER READING

ONLINE

For the reader who wishes to find out more about this fascinating case, a rich resource of documents and news articles is available online through the following links:

www.cbc.ca/news/background/baltovich_robert/index.html

www.cbc.ca/news/canada/story/2010/06/16/f-bernardo-homolka-timeline.html

INTERMEDIATE RESOURCES

Finkle, Derek. *No Claim to Mercy*. Toronto: Penguin Canada, 2004.

NEWSPAPER ARTICLES

Toronto Sun articles by Rob Lamberti (1990), Wendy Darroch (1992), Tracy Nesdoly (1992), Tracy Tyler (2000), Alan Findlay (2000)

Toronto Star articles by Wendy Darroch (1992), Tracy Tyler (2000), Betsy Powell and Peter Small (2008), Rosie DiManno (2008)

Globe and Mail articles by Thomas Claridge (1992), Kirk Makin (2000)

National Post articles by Derek Finkle (2000)

PHOTO CREDITS

We gratefully acknowledge the following sources for permission to reproduce the images contained within this book:

Robert Baltovich: cover, p. 61 (top and bottom), 62, 64 (top and bottom)

Jeff Mitchell: 63, 66

Pron, Nick. *Lethal Marriage*. Toronto: Seal Books, 1995. p. 65 (bottom)

Williams, Stephen. *Invisible Darkness*. Toronto: Little, Brown Canada, 1996. p. 65 (top)

INDEX

A

Annett, Stephen, 71
appeals, 71–80, 81, 91–92,
    97–98
arrest, 47–48
Association in Defence of
    the Wrongly Convicted
    (AIDWYC), 90, 91

B

bail hearing, 53, 91–92
Bain, Cathy, 41, 96
Bain, Elizabeth, 14–15, 17–21
    relationship with Rob, 16–
    17, 20–22
    diary of, 21–22, 27–28, 33,
    59–60, 71, 97
    disappearance of, 23–26
    search for, 26–29, 31
Bain, Julita, 25, 31–32, 44, 75,
    107
Bain, Ricardo, 31, 44, 107
Baltovich, Adele, 25–26, 49,
    85–88
Baltovich, Robert, 13–14, 18–
    19, 23–26, *61–64, 66*
    after prison, 11–12, 95–96,
    109, 112–13, 116–17
    arrest of, 47–48
    freed on bail, 53–54, 92–94
    in prison, 78–84, 86–87
    relationship with Liz, 16–17,
    20–22
    statements, 31, 35, 36, 59

Baltovich, Jim, *64*, 92
Bentley, Chris, 111
Bernardo, Paul, *65*, 97–104

C

Carter, Rubin "Hurricane," 91
charge to the jury, 72–73, 97
Claridge, Thomas, 56–57,
    67–70
Collins, Ruth, 68
compensation, 111–12
crime scene, 30, 102

D

defence. *See* Engle, Michael;
    Gatward, William; Lockyer,
    James
Dibben, David, 43, 57, 58, 102
DiManno, Rosie, 102–103, 108

E

Elliot, John, 68
Engle, Michael, 51–52, 55–56

F

Finkle, Derek, 83, 93
Fraser, Michael, 58

G

Gatward, William, 51–52, 55–
    56, 73
Genuis, Eric, 59

K
Kormos, Peter, 110
Kotanen, Phil, 105

L
Lockyer, James, 88, 89–92, 96, 106
Luke, Marnie, 74–75

M
McMahon, John, 57–60, 69, 71
media coverage, 32, 44–45, 47, 55, 56, 74–76, 83, 100–103, 107–108. *See also* Claridge, Thomas; DiManno, Rosie
Milhaven Penitentiary, 78–79

N
Nadon, Suzanne, 42, 43, 59

O
O'Driscoll, John, 72–73, 76, 97, 98
Ontario Court of Appeal, 79
Ormston, Ted, 51, 52

P
Perz, Marianne, 42–43, 57, 58
police investigation, 31–44, 47
Powell, Betsy, 100–102
preliminary hearing, 51–52
protective custody, 48–50
prosecution. *See* McMahon, John; Kotanen, Phil

R
Raybould, Brian, 31, 32–33, 40
Reesor, Steve, 31, 32–33, 39–40

S
sentencing, 76
Sherman, Vanessa, 41–42
Sicchia, Nancy, 71
Small, Peter, 100–102
statements, 31, 35, 36, 43, 59

T
Tonbazian, Naz, 96
transcripts, 36–38

V
verdict, 73–75, 105

W
Warkworth Institution, *62*, 80–84, 86–88
witnesses, 41–44, 51–52, 57–59, 68, 71
    hypnotism of, 43–44, 69, 114
Wozniack, Frank, 36–38, 59